The Scarecrow Press, Inc.
Metuchen, N.J., & London
1979

Anthony S. Jones
Lawrence W. Bagford
Edward A. Wallen

STRATEGIES
FOR
TEACHING

Library of Congress Cataloging in Publication Data

Jones, Anthony S   1941-
  Strategies for teaching.

  Bibliography: p.
  1. Teaching. 2. Lesson planning. 3. Audio-visual
materials. 4. Educational tests and measurements.
I. Bagford, Lawrence W., joint author. II. Wallen,
Edward A., joint author. III. Title.
LB1025.2.J66   371.3   79-20596
ISBN 0-8108-1257-6

ACKNOWLEDGMENTS

The authors wish to express deep thanks to Cathy Edwards for her responsible and patient typing of the manuscript. We appreciate being associated with such a fine and dedicated personality.

We want to give a special note of appreciation to our wives, Karen, Marilyn, and Gail, who lovingly endured the five years of sacrifice while we worked evenings and weekends on this text. Thanks, Ladies.

Tony, Larry, Ed

CONTENTS

STRATEGY: An educational method for turning knowledge into learning.

SUB-STRATEGY: Any medium which enhances the effectiveness of a teaching strategy.

INTRODUCTION

Methodological fluidity is the central theme of this book. We say this with a certain amount of apology for adding yet another mouth-filling piece of jargon to a field already overburdened with nouveau verbalisms, but we believe it essential in light of the lack of instructional flexibility (i.e., methodological rigidity) so pervasive in classrooms today. Despite the liberal atmosphere in American society today, such movements as accountability, competency-based education, and back-to-basics are reinforcing education's ever-present conservatism. An unfortunate spin-off of this trend is found in the routinized classroom where flexibility is erroneously viewed as incompatible with the amplified conservative emphasis of today. This is a serious judgmental error. The concept of "variety" is actually outside the liberal-conservative continuum of educational issues. Methodological fluidity refers to the ability of the instructor to better serve students' subject matter needs, and has nothing to do with undermining current trends or philosophies in education.

Teachers need to vary their teaching strategies in different classroom situations, but many competently utilize only a few, and many times only one. This severely limits the teacher's overall effectiveness. When a teacher relies upon a single approach (such as *drill* or *lecture*) as an instructional strategy, student boredom can easily create learning/discipline problems. A beginning psychology student who has studied brainwashing techniques knows the mentally aberrant effects of repetition and boredom. Fantasy, daydreaming, mental-dulling, and even hallucinations are natural outgrowths, and all beyond the individual's control (despite pleas from teachers to "Pay attention!"). A teacher's lack of methodological fluidity is indicative of a lack of knowledge of students' needs, interests and individual optimal learning conditions. It is, in effect, a very detrimental form of professional ignorance.

The purpose of this book is to illustrate graphically, in a straightforward manner, the different types of strategies (teaching methods) and sub-strategies (instructional media, or audio-visual aids) available to teachers attempting to expand their repertory of teaching tools. There are at least five solid reasons for a teacher being proficiently prepared in a wide assortment of strategies/sub-strategies:

1. Different students learn best in different ways at different times;

2. Some subject matter is best served by use of a particular strategy/sub-strategy or combination thereof;

3. Diverse objectives call for diverse approaches to meet the objectives;

4. The innate abilities of the teacher may determine the effectiveness of some strategies/sub-strategies; and,

5. Environmental factors (money, supplies, facilities, time, etc.) often dictate which strategies/sub-strategies will be most effective.

An Instructional Model

A short and simplistic model of instruction will illustrate the functional relationships of teaching strategies and sub-strategies to the total learning situation.

The instructional decision-making process demands that through observation, conversation, and evaluation of/with the students the teacher determines the needs, interests and individual learning styles pertinent to construct a viable learning module or lesson. A well-planned lesson includes objectives, instructional strategies and sub-strategies, and means of evaluating degrees of success in accomplishing objectives. This book is concerned with the total learning

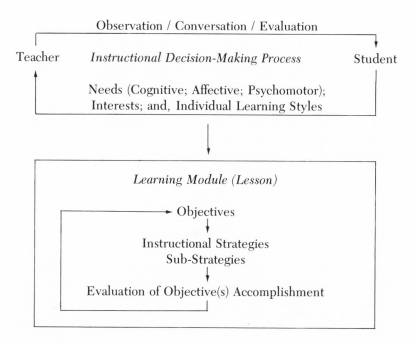

module (lesson) but places the heaviest emphasis on strategies and sub-strategies, or the body of the lesson. Further description is offered in the Planning for Teaching section of this chapter.

The mastery of instructional strategies is only one dimension of the skills, attitudes and knowledge needed by the competent teacher. For example, no amount of strategies can make up for lack of knowledge in subject matter. The converse is also true. The greater the teacher's knowledge of the subject, the more freedom he or she has to apply a variety of instructional approaches. The teacher should also have a basic understanding of philosophies of education, learning theory, and human development to act as a guide in the proper application of each strategy. The teacher must answer such questions as: What *is* a student? What are the student's needs, wants, and interests? What does a learner transfer from one experience to another? Any teaching strategy which is inconsistent with the student's desire for peer acceptance and approval is likely to meet with strong resistance. Even the most careful planning cannot produce beneficial results unless the student personally feels the need for learning. This requires consideration of the associated problems of providing adequately for individual differences. It is a rare student who will not create a disturbance (internally, if not externally) when class expectations are too high or too low for his/her capabilities. Yet, some teachers consistently expect all members of the class to read the same book, do the same problems and perform on the same level. As a result, these teachers often find their energies devoted to problems of class control. It is not that the teachers involved prefer a "lock-step" rather than an individualized curriculum; it is simply that they are at a loss as to how to go about creating the more desirable approach. It is hoped that this book will aid in that direction.

Utilization of This Book

Strategies and sub-strategies included herein are defined and described in their "pure form." After practice with a given strategy/sub-strategy has provided confidence in its use in the classroom, a number of strategies/sub-strategies can be combined and blended into new and creative patterns by the teacher. The knowledge, accuracy, and rapidity with which a teacher can apply strategies to a particular learning situation are some of the factors which differentiate the teacher as a technician and the teacher as a professional. Both stages are necessary, but one is a rung on the ladder to becoming the other.

The information in this publication is intended for a particular kind of reader: one who is interested in learning which teaching strategies/sub-strategies to use, when they can be used to best advantage, and why they should be used at a given point. This material is not intended to be a recipe book for all the ills of teaching. It is designed to aid and assist teachers in being more selective when choosing a strategy or sub-strategy for a particular educational purpose. It may help to reduce the overuse and possible abuse of the lecture method as a standard daily technique for many teachers and place this method in its rightful place: as a technique for transmitting information in an autocratic fashion to passive student listeners—a low-level cognitive function. Too often as teachers we tend to use that strategy which gives us a feeling of security. Consequently there is a hesitancy to employ more appropriate methods.

By understanding how different strategies/sub-strategies can best be used, we can benefit the students and ourselves.

Most curricular textbooks include some of the teaching strategies found in this publication. However, the efforts here have been directed solely to the compilation of selected teaching strategies. Each is presented in a systematic fashion to aid the reader in quickly determining its suitability or adaptability to a particular lesson. The organization and explanation for each teaching strategy has been uniformly developed and includes the following:

I. *Definition and Description*—briefly defines and/or describes the strategy and occasionally includes clarifying examples. It may also refer to other strategies which are explained in greater detail in a separate section;

II. *Advantages and Special Purposes*—includes a list of advantages or special purposes inherent in the strategy;

III. *Disadvantages or Limitations*—lists the disadvantages or limitations to consider before selecting a strategy or once the strategy has been selected. (Disadvantages should not be looked upon as deterrents, but rather as "preventive maintenance" problems to be overcome by practical planning.);

IV. *Guidelines for Maximum Utilization*—spells out some ways in which the strategy can be utilized with maximum efficiency;

V. *Summary*—a concluding statement; and,

VI. *Questions to Promote Discussion*—provides thought-provoking questions for teachers or future teachers.

The sub-strategy section (Part 2) includes sections I, II, III, and IV above, but not summary or question sections. It is suggested that sub-strategies be selected only after the teaching strategy for the lesson has been decided. This assures a more compatible and effective blend of instructional technique.

PLANNING FOR TEACHING

This book can improve one's ability to present viable and interesting lessons to students of any age, but selection of a strategy is *not* the primary step. A lesson may work out if the strategy is selected without pre-planning, but at best the results will be unpredictable. A good plan of action insures a greater probability of success while minimizing learning irrelevancy.

The teacher's plan of action is called a "lesson plan." The lesson plan is to the teacher what the blueprint is to the architect, the script to the director, and the flight plan to the pilot. It is a guide to assist the teacher and pupils in determining the direction of learning. It, like the three analogous examples, is time-consuming if done well.

The Lesson Plan

The lesson plan has three basic components. They include: (1) the objective(s), (2) the body of the lesson, and (3) evaluation. (A fourth component is sometimes included and is called "reteaching.") A brief discussion of each of the components is reviewed below to aid you in preparing lesson plans. (A rather extensive treatment of teacher-made tests is presented in Part Three).

Objectives

Benjamin Bloom and Robert Mager have repeatedly stressed the value of well-stated objectives in the planning of learning activities. As in planning a trip the first concern is, "Exactly where am I going?" The destination (objective) must be determined before further planning can be very effective. Further, the more specific the objective the easier it is to lay out a plan to accomplish it (e.g., tell a New York City cab driver, "Manhattan," when you really want to go to 542 Park Avenue, and see where you end up!).

In the lesson, what is it that the teacher hopes the pupils will learn? What do the pupils themselves want to learn? How well are they expected to achieve? These and similar questions form the basis of learning objectives. An example of an acceptable objective might read as follows:

> At the end of this lesson in mathematics, the student will be able to correctly divide a 4-digit number by a 2-digit divisor. Long division procedures will be used, carrying out the answer one place and rounding off to the nearest whole number. The student will correctly work 7 or more of the 10 problems assigned.

It should be clear to the teacher and the students just what is expected in this exercise. Both will know whether the lesson has been successfully carried out and whether any reteaching is necessary. Notice, again, how *specific* the statement of the objective is, and how much more direction it gives than: "The student will understand long division."

Body of the Lesson

The body of the lesson is the activity portion of the lesson. Having determined the objectives, one must then decide what methods or strategies can best enable accomplishment of those objectives.

Determining which teaching strategy to utilize is the choice of the teacher based upon: (1) knowledge of the learner's needs and/or interests; (2) school and classroom environmental constraints; (3) time and space considerations; and, (4) capabilities and limitations of the strategies themselves. The teaching strategy, the ability of the teacher to effectively utilize the strategy, and the pupils' ability and interest in the strategy-content combination will eventually determine the success or failure of the lesson.

Sub-strategies (instructional media) are enhancers of strategies. They can either support, amplify, or "decorate" a lesson to make it more attractive or magnify its impact. In many cases, they can make the difference between an effective lesson and a lemon. Sub-strategies are detailed in Part Two.

It is suggested again that the teacher become familiar with each strategy and sub-strategy in this book (first by study and then by using each one). This will provide an experiential and more accurate basis for strategy/sub-strategy selection.

Evaluation

Measuring accomplishment of learning is still one of the most controversial issues in education, and it always will be. A reason behind this is the depersonalization inherent in most forms of evaluation. For example, I can remember sweating through a course in statistics. Never did I study so hard or pile up so much frustration in one course before or since. Most memorable, however, is receiving the grade in the mail (No, I'm *not* going to tell you what it was!), staring at that little letter, and Peggy Lee's words running through my head like a repetitively taped message, "Is that *all* there is?" That evaluative designation said nothing of the long hours of study, the many days spent computing and solving long and arduous problems, the incredible amount of formula memorization, and the anxiety-producing test sessions. It did *not* describe how much I had achieved compared with what I knew at the beginning of the term. Nor did it describe how well I had done compared to the instructor's course objectives. But, *especially*, it did not portray the emotional obstacle course I had been forced to undergo. I resented it, frankly, like hell. Since then, however, my attitudes concerning the fairness and emotional aspects of evaluation have certainly been liberally expanded.

Evaluation does, of course, have other more meaningful forms than the test-for-a-grade one described. A good variation is exemplified by the long division sample objective. A properly written learning objective provides almost automatic evaluation. In the example previously given, if a student correctly completed 7 of the 10 problems, he/she has met the objective and is ready to move up in the division sequence. In other words, a well-written objective includes the evaluation component. Another example:

> The student will be able to diagram and label correctly the chambers of the human heart and illustrate with arrows the flow of blood through all four chambers.

This tells the student what the teacher expects him/her to learn, and, better still, how he/she must *demonstrate* that learning. This type of cognitive learning objective eliminates confusion and guesswork for both student and teacher. Further, it is "fair" in that the student is evaluated solely on the basis of the stated objective, rather than on peripheral learning the teacher feels the student should "probably" have internalized.

What is being discussed here is an alternative to tests as the only evaluative procedure. Ideally, a teacher has students performing demonstrable activities daily in all content areas. Accurate observation of everyday student performance is as valid an evaluative criterion of learning as is test-taking. Esler echoes this in his *Teaching Elementary Science* (Wadsworth Publishing Company, Inc., 1977):

> We have traditionally been victims of a test-culture, and teachers have shunned all but the test in evaluating progress of pupils. Hopefully, we are now breaking away from this fixation and are recognizing that the satisfactory completion of daily tasks may tell us more about a student than all of the tests he may take.

Classwide Evaluation

Instructional feedback for the purpose of improving teaching can be gained by analyzing the achievement of an objective by the total class. Did a number of students fail to achieve the objective? Were a number of students obviously disinterested or confused during the lesson? Were there students who failed to master any of the objectives? Affirmative answers to questions such as these should prompt the teacher to review how the lesson was taught:

a) Were the objectives clear and appropriate in relation to the ability of the class?

b) Had the students mastered the requisite skills and knowledge necessary to perform the lesson successfully?

c) Was the teaching methodology appropriate to the subject matter and student learning styles?

d) Was evaluation matched to the stated objectives?

It is establishment of this type of continual feedback loop that helps make teaching a profession and learning an enjoyable activity.

Summary

Lesson planning is time-consuming but rewarding in that it provides for accountability and repeatability of learning. The teacher and student both profit by having well-thought-out plans, as direction is provided without eliminating versatility or flexibility in presenting the lesson. Furthermore, the teacher has a viable opportunity to examine his or her own skills in relation to the skills of the students. The outstanding teacher has already learned this lesson well. The beginning teacher and those experienced teachers who have met with much difficulty previously should find good lesson planning one means of moving from a mediocre to an exceptional level of performance.

PART ONE

TEACHING STRATEGIES

BEHAVIOR MODIFICATION

Definition and Description

Behavior Modification is the term assigned to the application of laboratory-derived principles of learning to behavior problems which may be academic, social or emotional in nature. In practice, Behavior Modification may include such procedures as operant conditioning, contingency management, behavior modeling, role playing, and other planned techniques of attitudinal change.

Behavior Modification may also be known as behavior therapy or behavior management. It has been researched mostly with atypical children. However, the approach offers much for the teacher who desires to use the principles of operant conditioning to decelerate undesirable student behavior and accelerate desirable student behavior in the classroom.

Essentially, certain behaviors are established as desirable for students. Students who exhibit such behaviors, or who move in the direction of the prescribed behaviors, are rewarded, in the hope that this will increase the likelihood that the behavior will continue. The reward may be of a verbal nature (such as the teacher saying "good job"), material rewards, or an increase in student privileges.

A program in Behavior Modification should not be used as a panacea for all ills. It is a tool to be used selectively by the teacher. Indiscriminate use may bring about undesirable characteristics and/or neutralize the benefits later when the technique would have a role in changing the pupil's behavior.

Advantages or Special Purposes

1. The value of Behavior Modification has been scientifically demonstrated in classroom situations.

2. Behavior Modification is based upon tested principles of learning rather than theory.

3. Since Behavior Modification is concerned with observable, measurable behavior, both the student and teacher are aware of the amount of progress being made.

4. Behavior Modification is applicable to cognitive, affective and psychomotor learning.

5. The Behavior Modification approach leads to cooperation among the student, the teacher, the school and the mental health professional.

6. Since the emphasis is upon success, a positive atmosphere prevails.

7. The psychological principles involved can readily be learned by the classroom teacher.

8. The academic behaviors specified can be individualized very easily.

Disadvantages or Limitations

1. Not all behaviors to be learned can be measured.

2. Behavior Modification tends to have limitations where long-term retention is desirable.

3. A change in the student may not be based on desired learning but upon the rewards attached.

4. Care must be taken not to unintentionally reward undesirable behaviors.

5. The teacher may become emotionally involved with individuals and lose the effectiveness of the strategy.

6. Some techniques within the behavior modification strategy are extremely time consuming.

7. Behavior Modification requires some individualized type of plan. Giving the same reward to all students will negate the desired effect.

Guidelines for Maximum Utilization

1. Behavior Modification will not accomplish psychologically or academically impossible tasks.

2. The strategy should be used in conjunction with other learning strategies.

3. The behavior must be observable, measurable and controllable.

4. The Behavior Modification strategy must be understood and accepted by peers and parents.

5. The teacher must understand both the limitations and potential of the strategy.

6. After the child learns a new behavior, reinforcement should be tapered off and provided less frequently.

7. Although less reinforcement and reward are needed after the behavior has reached an acceptable level, occasional reward is necessary to maintain the behavior.

8. Continue to practice the Behavior Modification strategy in numerous settings.

9. Encourage parents to use discriminate reinforcement for events and behavior changes noted in the natural environment of the home.

10. Teach the child to manage his own behavior.

11. A learning environment must be created that will cause the child to engage in desired behaviors.

12. The objectives for each child must be realistic.

13. Introduce changes slowly.

14. The teacher should demonstrate those behaviors that are
    desired, and not assume that the child knows what to do.

Example

Mrs. Baker had a problem. Her second grade class could not
have been less enthused about spelling. She had tried the usual
thing: giving the children who did the poorest D's and F's on their
report cards. The low mark and parental pressure had worked in the
past, but this class was different. They didn't seem to be that
motivated by a low grade. Seeking enlightenment, Mrs. Baker
sought out the School Psychologist, Dr. Whizz, and told him of her
problem. Sizing up the situation quickly, the good doctor leaned toward Mrs. Baker and said, "Grades are based on the principle of de-
layed gratification. Children are just learning how to delay
rewards—a motivation system specialized in by adults only. Kids
want results now. Further, a letter grade is very abstract to a
child—he can't eat it, or play with it. Until children figure out the
'game,' a grade is just ink on paper. Related to this is the concrete-
abstract growth continuum. The younger a person the more concrete
his mental dealings. He wants tangible, hands-on action—*and* rewards. You must admit that spelling is abstract and relatively unim-
portant to an eight-year-old, besides being a rather boring bit of
business. Therefore, it is important for you to set up a system which
can make learning how to spell more concrete, more positive, and
more tangibly rewarding."

"First, if you're not already doing so, make the spelling words
as 'real' as possible. Label things in the room. Make up poems with
the words, etc. Then, set up a token system in addition to the
grades on spelling papers. Say, for every correctly spelled word the
child gets one token. At the end of the month children can exchange
tokens for items in a 'store' you set up with pictures, candy, gum,
toys, games, etc. Better still, allow them to utilize the tokens to buy
time in a game or music corner, in the comic book library, or arts
and crafts corner in your room. Does this help?"

"Yes, very much," Mrs. Baker replied, "I believe it will work."

And, of course, it did.

Summary

Behavior Modification is a teaching strategy that may be used in regular or special classrooms to modify behavior changes of a specified or desired nature. In its simplest form, it is a procedure whereby the instructor specifies through objectives the desired changes in pupil behavior and, when they occur, a reward is given to the student. In practice, however, it is a systematic process of observing the need for change, determining what changes are desired in each pupil, establishing objectives to carry out the changes and providing reinforcement or reward for those positive changes made. It must not be used indiscriminately; the program can have negative as well as positive results.

The strategy has been widely tested in laboratory situations and has gradually been instituted widely in public school systems. Positive results have been noted when it has been used by those who know and understand both the positive and negative effects that can result.

The use of this strategy in conjunction with *observation* skills, behavioral objectives, *individualized instruction, case study* and *programmed learning* can stimulate the students toward the desired behavior changes. It has also been used with a large degree of success in *role-playing* and *simulation* activities.

Questions to Promote Discussion

1. As can be readily seen, behavior modification focuses on behavior rather than personality. For example, if you are concerned about a student's tardiness you would say, "Tim, you have been 10–20 minutes late three of the last five school days," rather than, "Tim, you are just plain lazy. You never get to school on time." What are likely to be the effects on the student with this focus on behavior rather than on personality?

2. In Behavior Modification, the teacher should demonstrate the desired behavior so that the child will understand what is to be done. This means that the teacher serves as a model of desired behavior. What consequences do you see when you are cast in this model role?

3. What guidelines do you feel should be established concerning the granting of "rewards" for students who demonstrate a desired behavior?

4. What negative results can you expect if you grant rewards improperly to your students?

CASE STUDY

Definition and Description

The Case Study strategy (or case method) is a teaching approach which requires the student to participate actively in problem situations which may be hypothetical or real. He receives a "case," a report containing pertinent data, analyzes the data, evaluates the nature of the problem, decides upon applicable principles, and finally recommends a solution or course of action. The instructor has a wide range of choices of other strategies which may be included in the preparation of a case study technique.

The case may be considered by the class as a whole, by sub-groupings of the class, or on an individual basis. Also, the case may be designed to be handled in variable time-periods, ranging from a class period to the entire year.

The case can either be prepared for the student, which means there is a type of simulation or role-playing aspect of this strategy, or the student can garner his own data first-hand. Data should be objective and devoid of value judgment.

Analysis of the data typically involves the use of reference materials prepared for the study, knowledge, and theory already performed by others and listed in journals and books. It may, however, include *field studies*, personal or group *interview* and *research* activities.

Evaluating and determining applicable principles calls upon the student to make some kind of "reasons-why-this-has-happened" statement based on research or empirical observation. Recommended solutions should be a natural outgrowth of the analysis and evaluation. They should be practical and realistic.

There are numerous types of "cases." The most common (and, therefore, not displayed here) is the "individual case study," with which most social workers are familiar. It usually involves data on a single person or family, and necessitates that the case worker garner more pertinent information and recommend appropriate action based on problem causes.

A sample case prepared for your information:

CASE 1:   The Art Exhibit Problem

Purpose: The purpose of this technique is to add depth to the development of a better understanding of human relations. It makes us more aware of the total process an individual goes through as he/she attempts to make decisions, how he/she thinks and feels but does not usually express openly.

Note: A time limit of 30 minutes may need to be established to permit summary discussions to take place with the class as a whole.

Case Setting

This is a meeting of the art faculty representatives from the ABC School District. It is the regular meeting of the group conducted by the county supervisor. The problem to be discussed has been discussed in private by individual members of the art faculty, brought to the attention of the supervisor, and is of considerable concern to the administration. The administration is interested in increasing participation in the annual art show. The supervisor is aware that the faculty opinions range from a high degree of interest to those who are strongly against the show. The administration will accept the decision of the faculty.

Case Problem

Our art students are not participating in the annual art show. Should we encourage greater participation?

Case Participants

    1. *District Art Supervisor*
    2. *Elementary art teachers (5)*
    3. *Junior high school art teachers (2)*
    4. *Senior high school art teachers (2)*

Case Observers

    Observers are those members of the class not participating. They should consider the following questions and concerns.

    1. How do the participants function as a group?
      a. Conflict
      b. Leadership
      c. Expression of views

    2. Issues?
      a. Are they made clear?
      b. Do they recognize similarity of issues?
      c. Can they separate them from the problem?

    3. Conclusions?
      a. How do they arrive at conclusions?
      b. Are the conclusions satisfactory to the participants?
      c. Are they unable to arrive at a conclusion?

Summary—For Class Discussion

    The participants and observers should be asked for their reactions and comments to the proceedings, the questions raised and the outcomes and/or alternate solutions. The discussions should emphasize:

    a. How productive is the group and why?
    b. What are the problems and their solutions?

Advantages or Special Purposes

1. The Case Study approach can provide for individual differences among students.

2. Because the student is involved in a problem situation, interest and motivation are generally high.

3. Active student involvement insures better retention of content.

4. The Case Study approach develops responsibility on the part of the learner.

5. Students are invited to develop problem-solving skills in order to arrive at a conclusion to the case.

6. Realistic case studies bridge the gap between the "real" world and that of the school. As an example, the class might choose to study a problem involving their own school organization's operation (lunchroom, playground or class schedules).

7. Students deal with content on a high cognitive level.

8. Materials and resources other than the textbook are used in considering the case.

Disadvantages or Limitations

1. The Case Study approach can be time consuming.

2. Good case studies are difficult for the teacher to develop in a manageable procedure for the normal size class.

3. Resources and materials needed to pursue the case study successfully are often not available.

4. The teacher must be well prepared for the topic of the study.

5. Students may come to feel that all complex problems have rather simple solutions as experienced in the Case Study.

6. Cases are often what the teacher believes to be important rather than what the students see as important.

7. Cases developed by the students are often controversial and difficult for the teacher to manage.

8. Evaluation is difficult due to the open discussion or forum approach for group cases.

Guidelines for Maximum Utilization

1. Cases should be explicitly and unambiguously written.

2. Cases should be written to fit the level of the students in terms of maturity and problem-solving skills.

3. Students should be presented with several similar cases prior to permitting the students to select their own cases.

4. A check must be made to insure that materials and resources dealing with the case are available.

5. Check on students periodically to insure that they are progressing in a desirable direction.

6. Resist the temptation to solve the student's case. Let the student handle the case in order to benefit from the activity.

7. Establish a method and procedure for periodic and final evaluation prior to beginning the Case Study strategy.

8. Assist the student in evaluating the experience in terms of the content dealt with and the processes involved.

9. In cases that deal with controversial topics, clear the activity with the school administration prior to beginning the use of this strategy.

10. Attempt to include other strategies such as *role-playing, simulation, interview,* and *questioning* within the structure of the Case Study.

Summary

The Case Study method is another approach to individualizing the learning situation. Through the use of hypothetical or real situations, the student has the opportunity to use problem-solving approaches that are meaningful and understandable. It requires the student to collect data, analyze them and make suggestions or recommendations for decision-making. The project may be simple in the beginning and lead to the more complex as the student gains experience in these learning processes.

Using the Case Study strategy can, if it is properly directed, assist in the solving of school or community problems. The community sees the student working on topics that are of wide interest in the community and thus has greater respect for the educational programs at the local school. It further provides an opportunity to narrow the generation gap.

It is not a strategy to be used indiscriminately. It requires careful planning, specific objectives, clearly specified guidelines, and a precise means of evaluation. The teacher can and must expect to be available for individual assistance and must insure that materials, equipment and resources are readily available to the students. As with all other strategies, the school administration should be aware of the project and give the support to ventures which take the pupil outside the normal school environment.

Questions to Promote Discussion

1. What do you consider to be major difficulty in using the Case Study?

2. What suggestions do you have to overcome this major difficulty?

3. What, if anything, do the observers learn when the Case Study is used?

4. What do you consider to be the best use of the Case Study? Why?

COMMUNITY RESOURCES

Definition and Description

Basically, Community Resources include any activity outside the school which has educational use. Included, then, are *people, places,* and *things* found in the community which the teacher can use to facilitate learning.

The resource, although located outside the school building itself, may be brought to the school or the class may go to the site to carry out a planned activity. Often an elder citizen of the community can enhance the study of history or biology, art, folk dancing and literature. An insignificant dried up canal or creek bed can bring a wide variety of activities into focus. For example, a canal stream can be used to study the history, trade, transportation and economy of the past. It can also be used to study the plant life, become a collection area for artifacts, or be used as a model for the construction of science and art projects. The resources of the community are limited only by the imagination of the teacher and class. (See *field study* and *interview.*)

Advantages and Special Purposes

1. The use of Community Resources can bring the school and community closer together.

2. Community Resources can provide the student with first-hand knowledge and experience which facilitate more practical learning and better retention of information.

3. The use of Community Resources adds authenticity to learning since it involves contact with people, places or things outside the classroom walls.

4. Interaction between the school and community enables the student to develop a broader understanding of the community.

5. The use of Community Resources adds excitement to the subject, thus increasing motivation for learning.

6. Community Resources are applicable to all types of learning: cognitive, affective, and psycho-motor.

7. Students can develop social skills in helping plan and use Community Resources.

8. Students can assist in the selection of Community Resources as a decision-making experience.

9. Members of the community are generally willing to devote time and energy to these types of activities.

10. Community Resource activities are inexpensive and within the budgets of most schools.

Disadvantages or Limitations

1. Specific Community Resources are sometimes difficult to locate and/or schedule.

2. To use certain Community Resources, teachers must often obtain prior administrative and/or parental approval.

3. People used as Community Resources often do not know how to transfer their knowledge and information to youth.

4. Field trips into the community are often overlooked due to factors such as student safety, control, expense and teacher liability.

5. Improper use and planning for use of Community Resources can impede learning and create conflict between the school and community.

6. Proper planning of the use of Community Resources is time consuming and fraught with a series of legal and financial concerns.

7. The teachings of the community can run counter to the teachings of the school.

8. Since the teacher is dependent on agents of the community with primary responsibilities not essential to education, last-minute cancellations often occur, leaving the teacher stranded.

9. Rural areas may be handicapped by lack of access to museums, parks, business and industrial sites. Likewise, urban students will have limited access to the more rural types of Community Resources.

Guidelines for Maximum Utilization

1. Plan! Plan! Plan! Begin by developing a file of people, places and things in the community or in nearby areas which can be used to enhance instruction.

2. Check out each possible resource well in advance of its use.

3. Develop a resource file with information concerning procedures for use, necessary arrangements, people to contact, times the resources are available, size of groups that can be accommodated, etc., for each resource considered.

4. Investigate all legal, financial and economic factors involved for each resource considered.

5. Include the planned use of the resource in the total lesson or unit of study.

6. Present, in writing, the total unit or lesson to your administrator for approval. Having the plan in writing helps the administrator give approval.

7. Design a Plan B, in case of last-minute cancellations.

8. Upon completion of the lesson or unit, evaluate the resource utilized and place that information in the file for future use.

9. Put the knowledge gained to use as a part of the curriculum or lesson conclusion.

10. Don't forget to thank those persons who made the resource available.

Example

I.   A teacher advertised through an article in the paper for volunteers with various areas of expertise, hobbies, knowledge, etc., who would be willing to contribute an hour a week during the term. When she had screened the applicants, she furnished a list to her class to see who was interested in which area. As it turned out they were rather varied:

4 German Language
6 Chemistry
7 Photography
5 Arts and Crafts
6 Electronics

Each week the resource people came and took their "little brood" aside for intriguing projects and pastimes.

II.   Another teacher did approximately the same thing, but had the whole class choose one area for a month, and had a resource person in once a week for four or five weeks. Areas included: inventions, movie-making, archaeology, video-taping, music, hypnotism, fortune-telling, scuba diving, veterinary science, etc.

The first session was spent in establishing interests of the students in the area and a set of goal expectations based on these interests (and, of course, the expertise and resources of the guest instructor). Part of the final session was spent in evaluating the accomplishment of goals. Reports of new learnings were prepared by students and were sent home to parents. (See *interest centers.*)

Summary

Community Resources have an inherent place in the curriculum of all schools. Yet they are overlooked more often than not as a teaching tool in most educational systems. True, major industries, parks, museum and historical monuments are listed as places to visit. What about the people and places that are not nationally known but have a high educational value?

The teacher does not have to leave the school property to find a true resource. In many instances, teachers and other employees within the system have traveled and taken hundreds of slides and snapshots or brought back many souvenirs which if used by other classroom teachers could add new dimensions to the learning-teaching processes. Studies of the environment can be undertaken by studying the playground and surrounding areas. Sociological studies can be made by observing the people in action in or near the school. With a little imagination, even the classroom can be a resource.

Normally a community resource is considered to be something away from the school to visit, but in many instances it means bringing a person or exhibit to the school. Regardless of the definition, it is a tool that can provide new learning experiences to the class and assist the teacher in making lessons more meaningful and with lasting effects.

Community Resources, like all other teaching strategies, require advance consideration, study and preparation before they can become the meaningful tool they were designed to be. Begin early to note places of interest that will enhance the lesson. Make notes regarding the cost and the time needed to tour or complete the activity. Jot down the names of key individuals for contact and scheduling. Be knowledgeable about the procedures and requirements within the school for making use of Community Resources. Above all, have the objectives for using the resource firmly in mind to insure that the lesson is meaningful rather than using the community resource to fill in an unnecessary gap in the student's educational life.

Questions to Promote Discussion

1. What, in your estimation, is the reason Community Resources are used so seldom as a teaching strategy?

2. List some ways of overcoming the reason you stated in answer to Question #1.

3. The present emphasis on career education may well increase the use of Community Resources. If so, in what ways?

4. What advice concerning proper use of this strategy would you give to a teacher who has not previously used this approach?

CONTRACTING

Definition and Description

Contracting is a device in which a student and teacher together write exactly what is to be accomplished, in what period of time, and for what grade. The objectives are clearly specified, the work objectives outlined, and both teacher and student sign the written agreement (contract). Two copies are prepared so that the teacher and pupil can each keep one for reference and records. The contract itself is a written set of varied learning situations. Some are common to the entire class while others are individualized to meet the needs of the individual student.

To initiate the teacher in contract writing, a sample is provided. It may be modified to meet specific needs.

PERFORMANCE CONTRACT

For a Course in __Human Development_____

Name __Joe Dogood_____ Date __3/24/78_____

For the grade circled below, I am going to:	To exhibit my progress of these requirements, I will:
A — Do an original research project as explained on the attached sheet, plus completing all items for grade B, C, and D.	Submit the outline of my paper to the teacher by _____ (Date) and the completed paper by _____. (Date)
B — Perform a case study as explained on the attached sheet,	Submit the case study to the teacher by _____. (Date)

plus completing all items for
grade C and D.

C — Visit one of the following places   Submit a 1-page handwritten
and report my observations,   personal reaction paper to the
plus completing the materials   teacher by _____.
items for grade D.   (Date)
   a. Elementary School
   b. High School
   c. Mental Hospital (youth wing)
   d. Juvenile Detention Center

D — Read text of the course, *Human*   Passed examinations on:
Development and pass three (3)   _____
examinations;   (Date)
Be in class attendance 90 per-   _____
cent of the time; and,   (Date)
Write a one-page report on a   _____
topic of interest from the text.   (Date)

All exams and reports are graded pass or fail. If failed, they may be repeated. Please allow flexibility in your schedule.

_____   _____
Date   Student

_____   _____
Date   Teacher

_____   _____
Date   Parent (Optional)

Notice that in order to get a D in this course, the student must
read the text, write a one-page report, and get a "pass" on three
exams. In order to get a C, he/she must perform the requirements
for that grade, plus all requirements for the next lower grade. The
same holds true for the grade of B. If a student signs a contract for
an A at the beginning of the semester but for some reason completes
only the requirements for a B, he/she would get credit for what
he/she has accomplished.

Advantages or Special Purposes

1. The emphasis is on learning and success rather than testing and failure.

2. Students have a self-controlled opportunity for independence in their learning activities.

3. The relationship between students and instructor is improved because the student is not trying to "out-psych" the teacher and behavior problems are reduced or eliminated.

4. Cheating and duty-shirking are reduced.

5. The conditions for achieving a grade are clearly understood.

6. Communication is optimized as student and teacher *must* meet in regular individual conferences.

7. The learning objectives are clear to everyone.

8. Students can help select the projects rather than having the teacher pre-select the topic.

9. Varied experiences are insured. Students do not just "do more of the same activity" for a higher grade.

10. Students have choices, exercise decision-making abilities, and learn to organize and manage time.

11. Students may try, try again if they have difficulty (failure).

Disadvantages or Limitations

1. It is more work initially for the instructor than the straight "lecture" method or a question and answer session followed by a testing period.

2. Students can settle for grades below their "potential" (which, perhaps, should be their choice).

3. More record monitoring is necessary to insure that the students are keeping up with their schedules and are not having difficulties. This becomes necessary if the students have become used to educational spoonfeeding in the past.

4. "Quantity" may tend to replace "Quality" as a criterion.

5. The contract requires both in-school and out-of-school resources, which may be difficult to locate.

6. Some students are not mature enough to fulfill the contract responsibilities or lack the self-motivation required for this strategy.

Guidelines for Maximum Utilization

1. Preparation of objectives must always come first. What do you wish the student to learn? What does the student wish to learn? What are the best methods to achieve the objectives? What are the best criteria to use in judging whether the student has achieved the objectives?

2. Insure that all materials, resource people and places necessary to carry-out the contract are available.

3. Draw up contracts based on Items 1 and 2 of the guidelines.

4. When you have your contractual agreement sessions, students must understand the necessity of self-motivation, time schedules and material needs. Include adequate time for "re-trials" in the event that students are not successful on tests and reports.

5. Remember, the contract does not eliminate the need for daily class activities. It is supplemental or in addition to regular class work.

6. Clearly establish the level of acceptance on papers and exams. Since students get either a "pass" of "fail" on tests, you need to determine the pass-fail line (75%, 80%, etc.).

7. Once the contract is signed, it is binding upon both the teacher and student. Keep your word.

8. As result of experiences, revise your procedures, contracts, objectives, etc. Continuously sharpen up the process and keep it updated.

9. Before beginning this strategy, be certain it has the approval of the school administration.

10. Repeated use of this strategy for every lesson or unit will weaken its effectiveness. Attempt to use it in selective situations and blend use of other strategies within the contract.

Summary

The Contracting strategy is a stepping-stone into the individualized learning processes. The contract is written to meet the needs of each individual, based on objectives of both the student and the teacher. The level of acceptable achievement must be based on more than the general expectations of the class. Considerations must include the maturity of the students, previous experiences in contracting, the ability to carry out tasks on an individual basis, and the challenge to both the teacher and the student.

Contracting is not a strategy that once assigned leaves the teacher free from all daily planning and teaching. Quite the contrary, it requires the teacher constantly to monitor progress through individual conferences, to assist students in finding the needed resources, and to keep regular records of attendance, progress and testing.

The contract can be an elaborate document or a simple written statement of agreement between the student and the teacher. The important part of this strategy is the opportunity it gives students to learn while doing a project that the students have selected with teacher approval. It is a chance for the student to experience success and failure, yet provides the opportunity to try again without the feeling of complete failure.

It is important to clearly establish administrative approval before beginning this strategy. Since some of the contracts may require leaving the school environs to visit a community resource, parents should also be aware of the activity and understand the concept of contracting. With parental support and administrative approval, the teacher insures positive chances of success.

Questions to Promote Discussion

1. Luke Lance is going to teach the sixth grade in a school system which utilizes the self-contained classroom. Luke wants to try contracting. Do you recommend that Luke begin the method with one specific subject or with all subjects at the same time? Why?

2. You have decided to use contracting and all involved people agree it is a good idea. Upon implementing the approach, your best student decides to settle for a C. What would your reaction be? What would you do?

3. Also, in Problem 2, your most "marginal" student decides to shoot for an A. What would your reaction be? What would you do?

4. In facing the situations in Problems 2 and 3 above, were you consistent? In what ways? Did any inconsistencies appear in your thinking? If so, what were they?

DEMONSTRATION

Definition and Description

Demonstration is the process wherein one person does something in the presence of others in order to show them how to do it or to illustrate a principle. Demonstration utilizes both auditory and visual means of communication.

Advantages or Special Purposes

1. Demonstration adds to learning by giving students the opportunity to see and hear what is actually happening.

2. Demonstration can be used to illustrate ideas, principles, and concepts for which words are inadequate.

3. *Good* Demonstrations hold the learner's attention.

4. Demonstrations can be financially economical since only the demonstrator needs materials.

5. Students can conduct Demonstrations, thus building associated skills and attitudes.

6. Demonstrations can reduce hazards before students begin experimentation or operation with materials involved (especially true in science labs, shops, or home economics classes).

7. Demonstrations lead to a reduction in the length of trial-and-error time.

8. *Good* Demonstrations set performance standards (which can be inspiring in such fields as arts and crafts, music, typing, physical education, etc.).

9. Demonstration is especially beneficial in the areas of skills.

10. Demonstration is an excellent technique for utilizing community resource persons which in turn is good for public relations.

Disadvantages or Limitations

1. Demonstration can require much planning and preparation by the demonstrator.

2. A Demonstration can be ineffective if the demonstrator only "shows and tells," without feedback.

3. The Demonstration approach cannot be properly used in large classrooms or with extremely small objects because all students cannot see.

4. If the audio portion of the Demonstration does not fit (flow with) the visual portion, it can confuse the student.

5. Demonstration can lead to imitation without understanding.

6. Demonstration can lead to "oversimplification" of the complex, which can result in feelings of failure or inferiority when students cannot "measure up."

7. Demonstration is difficult to use with affective and higher-level cognitive learnings.

8. Several Demonstrations become time consuming.

Guidelines for Maximum Utilization

1. Spend the necessary time to plan and develop the needed materials for the Demonstration.

2. Practice or rehearse the Demonstration in its entirety with an eye on time limitations.

3. When it is time to put on the Demonstration make sure that all materials are at hand.

4. Make sure seating arrangements are such that the audience can see and hear.

5. Utilize questions during the Demonstration to provide feedback.

6. It often helps to discuss and demonstrate the "wrong way" to perform a task as well as the "right way" (e.g., "Look what happens when too much water is added while forming this ceramic pot on the wheel").

7. At the conclusion of the Demonstration, conduct a brief review of the steps involved or a short summary of what has happened.

8. If feasible, have a student or two replicate the Demonstration.

Summary

One of the greatest benefits of Demonstration is showing how something is accomplished properly or expertly. Naturally, then, the Demonstration should be properly prepared to ensure that this goal is achieved. A good Demonstration inspires, a poor one distracts and demotivates.

Demonstration is especially useful in the arts, music, science, mathematics, and athletics. It is commonly used in conjunction with a short explanatory lecture.

Questions to Promote Discussion

1. Why is a good Demonstration a really powerful means of teaching?

2. In your estimation, in what way is Demonstration often misused?

3. What do you consider the key element in using Demonstration properly? Why?

DISCOVERY (INQUIRY)

Definition and Description

Discovery is a term which connotes different meanings to different people. Basically, Discovery is a teaching strategy which enables students to find the answers themselves. In Discovery students are involved in learning how to learn.

In practice, directed Discovery is used more than pure Discovery as the teacher generally creates the conditions under which the "discovery" is to occur. In essence, "discovery" is really "re-discovery." The intent is that students will discover for themselves that which has been previously discovered.

In implementing Discovery, the teacher creates a situation in which the student is faced with a problem. In solving the problem, the student uses raw data and behaves in the manner required by the nature of the discipline and the problem. Thus, the student studies history the same way that a historian does or as a biologist studies biology.

Advantages or Special Purposes

1. Since the student actively discovers the information and knowledge, retention will be increased.

2. Discovery helps the student learn how to follow leads and clues, and to record findings, thus equipping him/her to handle new problematic situations.

3. The rewards inherent in discovering something provide the student with intrinsic motivation.

4. The student develops further interest in what is being studied.

5. Students develop the skills and attitudes essential for self-directed learning.

6. Students develop a deeper understanding of the tasks of a scholar.

7. Discovery operates at the higher levels of the cognitive domain (analysis, synthesis, etc.); it also encourages intuitive thinking.

8. The pupil is provided with numerous opportunites to draw inferences from data by logical thinking, either inductive or deductive.

Disadvantages or Limitations

1. Permitting students to discover their own knowledge is very time consuming. It is inefficient to expect students to re-discover or recreate all knowledge.

2. Most of the present textbooks and materials available to the teacher are written for exposition rather than Discovery.

3. The student often gets bogged down or loses direction before the problem is solved.

4. Students often discover things other than what was intended to be "discovered."

5. An erroneous Discovery following great effort can be extremely deflating for the student.

6. The teacher must have a strong background in the subject to handle unexpected discoveries.

7. Some students just seem unable to make the intended Discovery.

Guidelines for Maximum Utilization

1. Discovery should be used only when you have enough subject matter mastery to handle unexpected "discoveries."

2. The depth of information to be handled and the time needed for the Discovery must be gauged in terms of the student's skill level and maturation and the objectives of the course or subject.

3. Setting up the problem and the conditions for Discovery requires detailed and thorough planning.

4. Be certain that proper materials and raw data are available.

5. Be open to problems as they arise and be willing to learn along with the students.

6. Upon conclusion of the Discovery experience, spend time reviewing and/or evaluating the experience in terms of both the knowledge learned and the processes involved.

7. Permit students to share discoveries with the class to extend the learning environment.

Example

To give the class an opportunity to use Discovery (Inquiry), present the following situation to small groups within the class. It is a form of *simulation* but requires the student to use data, accept or reject positions of others and arrive at a conclusion.

HOSPITAL ADVISORY BOARD

You are a Hospital Advisory Board. There is one available Kidney Dialysis Machine in your hospital. You have ten people who must be hooked up to the dialysis machine one hour from now or they will die. But, of course, *only one can live*. Your task: Select the one who will live (or the nine who will die).

A. Male Heart Surgeon; Age 55; Married; No children.
B. Male Insurance Salesman; Married; 2 Children; Age 32.
C. Male Hippie; College drop-out; Age 20; Single.
D. Female Elementary School Teacher; Married; 1 Child; Age 27.
E. Black Minister; Age 58; Married; Children Grown-up.
F. 16 year-old Girl.
G. Female Black Militant; Divorced; 2 Children; Age 26.
H. Male College Student; Married; No Children; Age 22.
I. Retired Air Force Colonel; Single; Age 49.
J. Male Politician; Age 36; Married; 4 Children.

Procedure: 1. Use any method of selection your group decides upon together.

2. Turn in one paper with all your names on it.

3. Rank-order your selection of the ten in order of the one that should be allowed the use of the machine first. (That way, in case the first one for some reason cannot use the machine, you will have a second choice ready.) The last one on the list should be in your minds the last one to be "saved."

4. Explain why you picked #1 as you did. Please be specific about criteria utilized.

Sample Follow-Up Questions for the Teacher

1. How much time was wasted fighting the problem? What implication does this have for our everyday lives?

2. What prejudices surfaced?

3. Was there "sense" in establishing the selection criteria?

4. Was the selection process humanely done?

5. Did a leader evolve in the group?

6. Was the leader fair (unbiased)?

7. What comments made during the simulation turned you off?

Summary

The thrust of Discovery, as with the Socratic method, is that answers, or the potential for discovering answers, are inherent within the student. This requires the teacher to guide the process patiently until the "revelation" occurs. A very good example is illustrated in Postman and Weingardner's *Teaching as a Subversive Activity* (although the example is labeled "Inquiry"). A social studies teacher brings a small black briefcase to class, explaining that it is the world's smallest computer, and that it will answer any question the students ask—but only one. An earnest discussion (that lasted for days) ensued as to which question to ask. Values had to be shared, attitudes and ideas exchanged, and priorities arrived at to determine *the* question. Once the teacher had "set the stage," it was the students' show and the teacher merely acted as a type of social and structural referee.

Discovery is frequently used in science and math, but is relevant for most other subject areas as well. The teacher provides the materials and the students provide the discovering. Some pure form Discovery strategists accept all discoveries, stating that there is no *right* answer. This is more of a process approach as opposed to the usual emphasis in education on production.

Questions to Promote Discussion

1. What is the major advantage of the Discovery approach? Explain.

2. What is the chief limitation of the Discovery approach? Why?

3. How would you attempt to overcome the limitation cited in response to Question #2?

DISCUSSION

Definition and Description

The *Dictionary of Education* describes Discussion as:

> an activity in which people talk together in order to share information about a topic or problem or to seek possible available evidence or a solution. . . .

Discussion may be implemented in a variety of ways. The types of Discussion available to the teacher include whole-class discussions, debates, panels, buzz-sessions, and forums. Each type has its own characteristics.

The whole-class Discussion is the type generally referred to when teachers employ the discussion method. The teacher simply leads an informal Discussion involving the class as a whole. The teacher, as the director of the Discussion, asks questions, clarifies student comments, and makes tentative summaries to help students achieve understanding of the topic.

Debate is generally used in the classroom as a small-group technique, with a small number of students teamed on either side of an issue. Each side is given a specific amount of time to present its "side" of the issue. The members can alternate presentations and often are identified as "pro" and "con" with respect to the issue. Rebuttals of a specific time duration then follow the presentations. Upon conclusion of the debate, the teacher can enter into a whole-class discussion on the issue.

In utilizing *panels*, the teacher can divide the class into groups of three to six students. The students comprising the panel then organize themselves, research the topic, discuss their data, and then present their findings that lead into a whole-class discussion.

In *buzz sessions*, students are placed in small groups for a specific amount of time to discuss a given issue or topic. Reports of the results of the various buzz groups are then presented to the entire class and stimulate whole-class discussion.

The *forum* is a specific Discussion type in which a small number of students present information to the larger group. Upon the conclusion of the presentation, the presenters then solicit questions on the topic from the audience. This puts the presenters in the role of "authorities" on the topic and questions may be directed to specific members of the group of "experts."

The types of Discussion approaches listed above represent only the most commonly used. Each of the types presented can be used in either a modified form or in combination with each other. Whatever the case, teachers should use the approach properly in terms of its inherent characteristics.

Advantages or Special Purposes

1. Students learn through Discussion. Not only do students learn the cognitive information considered, they utilize the information in a meaningful manner and thus reach the higher levels of the cognitive domain.

2. Discussion techniques get at attitude development. By engaging in meaningful discussion with fellow students, a given student finds his/her own values and beliefs challenged. Such a finding can lead to significant attitudinal change on the part of the student.

3. Discussion provides the student with the opportunity to develop questioning skills and responses. It offers an opportunity to develop organization and formulation of answers. In essence, the student begins to think and organize on his/her feet.

4. The proper use of Discussion can aid the student in the development of a positive self-concept.

5. The student is free to offer or not to offer comment.

6. Discussion has a positive effect upon the mental activity of the student. Since the role of the student is not as passive as with some other approaches, the student maintains a high degree of mental alertness. This alertness is one reason why discussion is often praised as being a motivator.

7. Discussion provides the teacher with information about the student which can aid in a better understanding of students, individually and collectively. Careful observation of the behavior of students in group activities provides the teacher with much information related to the social, psychological, emotional, and skill development of the student.

Disadvantages or Limitations

1. Discussion activities are usually time consuming compared with more direct approaches.

2. Discussions often break down, lag, or become a rambling, meaningless "pooling of ignorance."

3. In Discussion, some students may never participate while a few may tend to dominate.

4. Long and/or frequent periods of silence can occur in a Discussion. Such silence often leads the teacher to take over the class in pursuit of the topic.

5. Whether or not the class members will get into a Discussion on the topic is always a risk.

6. It is possible that a topic will be such that the students get carried away. They might lose self-composure, get too emotionally involved, and let matters get completely out of hand.

7. Teachers often become frustrated because Discussion may fail to lead to a conclusion, or at least to the conclusion the teacher believes to be most desirable.

8. Students often lack the informational background or maturity to contribute to a meaningful Discussion.

9. Finally, there is the problem of evaluating the student. How does one accurately measure the contribution of a given student to the Discussion?

Guidelines for Maximum Utilization

1. An atmosphere of "acceptance" must exist in the classroom. If the classroom atmosphere has in the past been one of hostility and strain between the teacher and students, Discussion will not work. Students must feel free from threat in order to speak openly.

2. The teacher must be prepared. The teacher must be familiar with the content to be considered, the characteristics of group activity, and the materials and resources available to the students.

3. The students must be prepared. In order to insure that the Discussion reaches a level higher than a "sharing of ignorance," the teacher must plan sufficient learning activities prior to the Discussion.

4. Discussion should be used when teacher objectives are considered worth the extra time required. Generally, the objectives appropriate for the Discussion process would involve higher-level cognitive learning, affective learning, and skill learning related to Discussion.

5. The topics for Discussion should be properly stated. Primarily, the topic should be stated as an issue, if possible, to "polarize" viewpoints. Secondly, the words used to phrase the issue should be terms familiar to the students. Finally, the topic itself should be one which has some degree of personal relevance for the students.

6. In introducing the subject matter to be discussed, the question or issue should be presented in very specific, well-defined terms

to the students. In fact, writing the topic on the board or in hand-out material is well worth the effort.

7. In introducing the topic, take time to clarify terms and establish the relevance of the topic.

8. Use panels, forums, debates, or buzz-sessions on occasion to lead up to whole-class Discussion. These take time to organize and plan, but the variety can help motivate, and there is the assurance that at least a few students will be prepared.

9. The teacher serves as moderator of the Discussion while it is in progress. The moderator clarifies concepts, makes tentative summaries, states conclusions, and keeps the Discussion on track.

10. Respect silence and the contribution it can make. Learn to discern the nature of the silence. If the silence is due to the fact that students are thinking, they should be allowed to think. If the silence is due to confusion, clarify the last question or summarize the Discussion up to that point.

11. Encourage many students to participate, but do so unceremoniously. A question directed to a specific student or a simple "What do you think, John?" will suffice. Realize that not every student will need to have something to say on every topic. Be satisfied that several students may discuss any given topic, and that all participated over several topics at one time or another.

12. Discourage dominance by a few by handling the situation privately. Merely inform the rambunctious students that you appreciate their efforts and want them to continue, but that others need to be heard from too. If this does not do it, a little more direct statement needs to be made in private.

13. Always have a summary when the Discussion is over. This may be done by the teacher or by the students. The Discussion has been in vain if the students are unaware of the conclusions reached, positions taken on the issue, or processes undergone.

14. Look for follow-up activities. Successful Discussion will lead naturally into follow-up activities which will enhance the student's learning.

15. Unless specified as a designed objective, student Discussion should not be evaluated for grading purposes. This is the only way to encourage students to contribute freely and honestly to the discussion. To use participation in the Discussion as a factor in grading only encourages the student to "psych-out" the teacher and then provide the desired answer.

Summary

Discussion is a most important strategy on a number of levels. First, it does involve the coverage of academics. Secondly, it involves a sharing of ideas *between students*, rather than an osmotic process from teacher to student. Thirdly, it is a schooling in social interaction, courtesy, leadership/followship, thought organization, and conversation. In this last level is the preparation for students to become proficient speakers/listeners and worthwhile contributing citizens—a goal found in every school philosophy.

Discussion does demand supervision and guidance by the teacher. One well-known killer of effective Discussion is "rambling" or "loss-of-target" talking. This is a sure sign of boredom or lack of direction and calls for teacher interference in an appropriate manner. The lack-of-knowledge problem which results in ineffective Discussion demands that the teacher be prepared to point out bolstering, relevant resources.

Questions to Promote Discussion

1. From your experiences, is Discussion a worthwhile strategy to use? Why or why not?

2. Why is it essential for the teacher to think about Discussion in terms of both "content" and "process"?

3. What is the major reason so many Discussions turn out to be unproductive?

4. What are the most important guidelines to be used that will ensure a productive Discussion? Why?

DRILL

Definition and Description

Although there are many sub-types, Drill is "a teaching technique intended to bring about automatic accuracy and speed of performance in any subject." The aim of Drill, then, is the fixation of correct information or skill through repetition.

Some use the term "drill" only for mental ideas and "practice" for motor activity. However, since both are built on repetition—doing it over and over—"drill" and "practice" will be used here synonymously.

Advantages or Special Purposes

1. Drill is especially applicable in psychomotor (skill) and low-level cognitive learning.

2. Some knowledge cannot be retained by a single exposure, thus requiring Drill (e.g., multiplication tables).

3. In skill development, repetitious practice is essential to build competence and technique mastery.

4. Students can build their own associations of information through Drill.

5. Used in student tutorial situations, it can be a means of creating motivation.

6. Slower students can be used as tutors.

7. Affective learning can take place by grouping the slow and fast achievers as a drill team.

8. Drill can be used in time allotments of short duration when no other activities are planned.

Disadvantages or Limitations

1. Drill can become boring and monotonous.

2. Information acquired through Drill will not be retained long without use.

3. Overuse of Drill can lead students (*and* teachers) to believe in memorization as an end.

4. Drill can reduce learning to a purely mechanical act.

Guidelines for Maximum Utilization

1. Use Drill only when automatic speed and accuracy or performance learning is the objective.

2. Make sure students understand the purpose of the Drill or practice.

3. Use both individual and group "concert" exercises.

4. Use games and contests to add interest to Drill.

5. Make sure students are practicing with correct information or processes. It is only *correct* practice which makes perfect.

6. Organize Drill periods with regard to proper spacing and length of Drill time. Over-practice produces boredom and fatigue.

7. Provide the opportunity for students to apply that which is mastered through Drill.

Summary

The function of Drill is solely to create automatic responses to specific stimuli. If you were effectively drilled in multiplication and someone came up behind you and said quickly, "What's 9 × 9?" your response should be "81"—instantly, without thinking about it. Football drills in throwing an effective block are designed to teach the player to do it automatically. So are bayonet drills in the armed services, and instruction in memorizing the capitals of the United States. It is a practice closely paralleled by programming a computer. The teacher should remember that this is the only purpose of Drill. It has nothing to do with elevating mental functioning or making better citizens. Overused, Drill is a surefire method of dulling cognitive abilities and promoting discipline problems. The percentage of class time spent on Drill exercises should be minimal.

Questions to Promote Discussion

1. Is the statement "Practice makes perfect" a true one? Why or why not?

2. Does Drill belong in the teacher's kit of strategies? Why or why not?

3. Explain the chief disadvantages of Drill.

4. What is the most important guideline for the successful use of Drill? Why?

FIELD STUDY (TRIPS)

Definition and Description

The Field Study is "a trip arranged by the school and under-taken for educational purposes, in which students go to places where the materials of instruction may be observed and studied directly in their functional settings."

A sub-function of the *community resources* strategy, Field Studies are generally made to points of instructional interest such as factories, public utilities, museums, libraries, art galleries, or government installations. They may also include scientific forays to streams, ponds, fields and forests, to collect specimens for immediate or future studies.

Advantages or Special Purposes

1. Field Studies provide the student with interesting, first-hand experiences.

2. A common experience is provided for students which can serve as a basis for other learning activities.

3. Students become more aware of their environment.

4. Field Studies can add greatly to school-community relationships.

5. What is learned should have great impact due to the multi-sensory nature of the experience.

6. This procedure can be utilized by teachers of any and all subject areas in the curriculum.

7. Field Studies extend classroom learning through reality.

8. Field Trips are a change of pace from constant classroom activities.

Disadvantages or Limitations

1. The legal responsibilities accompanying a Field Study are serious.

2. Discipline can easily become a problem.

3. Administrative procedures to organize Field Trips are often so complicated that they discourage taking them.

4. Transportation arrangements are often difficult or costly.

5. When a teacher has students for only one period a day, it is difficult to make arrangements which do not create conflicts with other classes.

6. Field Trips require additional chaperones and these may be difficult to secure.

7. If not properly planned, the Field Study becomes a waste of time and takes away from valuable learning activities.

8. An improperly planned trip may deter other teachers, and place doubt in the mind of the administration about the value of this strategy.

Guidelines for Maximum Utilization

1. Before even considering the Field Trip, become familiar with the legal aspects of teacher liability involved.

2. Make sure the Field Trip is of educational value in that it relates directly to what is being taught in the classroom.

3. Plan the Field Trip by visiting the site and talking with the people before actually making the decision to undertake the Field Study.

4. Obtain permission from school authorities.

5. Make all transportation arrangements.

6. Notify parents to obtain consent. Parents often like to go along, giving added supervision as well as driving help.

7. Prepare the class by relating the trip to what is being studied and what they might observe.

8. Establish safety, dress and behavior standards.

9. At the site, provide for adequate supervision.

10. Be sure all students are where they are supposed to be.

11. Handle small incidents as they occur. Do not let unsafe behavior continue.

12. Upon return to the classroom, review and summarize what was learned on the Field Trip.

13. Have the class send a "thank you" message to the hosts of the Field Trip.

14. Develop a means for evaluating pupils and the place visited in order to assist in planning future trips.

Summary

One of the long-standing major criticisms of education has been its sponsorship of cloistered, unrealistic learning of irrelevant facts. Field Study is a means of overcoming this criticism in part. It provides opportunity for students to see the "real world" in action, and, thereby, widens their attitudinal, social, and academic horizons.

Careful planning and pre-visitation to the site by the teacher is essential if the experience is to be useful and valuable to students. Undoubtedly, thousands of field trips have been a wasted, futile experience because of insufficient pre-planning. Students should receive some definite "coaching" in observation skills and an outline of objectives and purposes prior to the Field Trip. Follow-up activities including discussion, writing short essays, drawing pictures, or model-making will ensure that retention of the objectives is accomplished.

Field Study, properly carried out, is a major source of enrichment for learners.

Questions to Promote Discussion

1. What do you consider the major value of a Field Trip? Why?

2. What do you consider the chief drawback of the Field Trip? Why?

3. Do you feel the answer to Question #1 outweighs the answer to Question #2, or vice versa? Why?

4. What would you do if, at the last moment, the parents of a student in your class refused to let their child participate in a planned field trip? Is your suggested solution fair to all involved?

FUTURISTIC FORECASTING

Definition and Description

Futuristics is the process of projecting into the future and attempting to forecast what noteworthy events will take place; what the world and its people will be like; where our food, clothing and housing will come from; how society in general may function to maintain a safe and peaceful world, etc.

As an example, a student or group of students may undertake the problem of transportation. What form will it take? With the present pollution problems, what form of fuel will be used to eliminate pollution and its ill effects on society? What effect will the movement of the population to the outlying areas of large cities have on the choice of transportation? These and many more areas could be included in the study of this type of problem under the heading of Futuristic Forecasting.

This strategy, properly used, requires a combination of skills. *Research, field trips, community resources* and *individualized study* permit the student to be creative in a useful way.

Futuristic Forecasting is a form of directed daydreaming. It requires supportive data, logical thinking, statistical study and good analytical skills. It is a strategy that can be used in almost any subject area and yet it supports and enforces the basic skills of reading, writing and mathematics.

Advantages or Special Purposes

1. It is an opportunity to study socialization in such a way as to make individuals question the status quo.

2. It permits continuous change and frequent modification and/or abandonment of courses and units of learning experiences.

3. Futures forecasting is, or can be, an individualized learning tool.

4. It is an opportunity for students to specialize in an area of their choice.

5. Futuristics helps to prepare students to become researchers, developers, disseminators and/or practitioners.

6. It provides students an intensive choice in the selection of one area to intellectually challenge their interests.

7. It expands the school learning environment by requiring facilities outside the classroom and/or building.

8. The opportunity to use a wide range of resource persons and consultants is made possible in this strategy.

Disadvantages or Limitations

1. All studies and changes are based on the assumption of uncertainty.

2. Teachers may fear to delve into the area of the unknown.

3. The school administration may frown on teachers leaving the approved curriculum to study the unknown.

4. Technological facilities may not be available (either in the school or in the nearby community) to carry studies far enough into the future to be of worthwhile value.

5. Students who have been programmed in the traditional ways of learning may not be sophisticated enough to pursue the unknown.

6. Very little information is available to study the future and the student who is unable to locate necessary information to complete the study may lose interest.

Guidelines for Maximum Utilization

1. Enter this strategy with caution and with a short-term project in the beginning.

2. Ensure a complete understanding and acceptance by all parties concerned (school administration, parents and pupils) prior to beginning studies in futuristics.

3. Develop a clear set of objectives for yourself and have the students do likewise at the outset of a futuristic study.

4. Once the process is begun, allow the students to think "far out." Remember, Buck Rogers was 25 years ahead of our first space orbit.

5. Attempt to foresee what resources will be needed and if they are available locally.

6. Direct student projects and studies into categories useful to mankind, i.e., food production needs, mobility of society, transportation requirements of mass populations, land use, etc.

7. Keep an open mind. Do not attempt to limit students' thinking, as the projected changes are based on assumptions of uncertainty.

8. Guide and direct the pupils, but don't dictate.

Summary

Who knows at this time what the future holds in store for mankind? With the advent of the nuclear age, there is much room for uncertainty.

This strategy offers the opportunity for students and teachers to dream, to think, and to play games regarding what they believe the world will be like in the year 2001 and beyond. It allows the opportunity to forecast without being hurt or penalized for making wrong forecasts or conclusions. It is a form of simulation gaming.

Certainly there were those among us who had not dreamed that Neil Armstrong or anyone else would walk on the moon. Why not allow students to forecast what they see in the future and attempt to support their theories? This strategy will expand their creative thinking, their research skills and their ability to find support for their beliefs. It is a combination of strategies including *research, demonstration, individualized instruction, field study, community resources* and many others. What the students forecast now may in actuality come true in our lifetime—or at least in theirs.

Questions to Promote Discussion

1. What subject areas seem most suited to Futuristic Forecasting? How?

2. How would you structure a forecasting session, i.e., introduction, guidelines, rules, resources, summary?

3. Resources are important to the success to Futuristic Forecasting. List all the potential resources you could have access to in your particular situation.

INDEPENDENT STUDY

Definition and Description

Independent Study is an arrangement whereby the student explores in depth an area of interest not normally studied by the entire class. At the post-secondary level, Independent Study is often used when there is a conflict in schedules or to cover a required subject not presently being offered. The topic to be explored can be assigned by the teacher or selected by the student with the teacher's approval. The aim is to provide a unique learning experience for the student. (See *student research*, *project*, and *laboratory*.)

Advantages or Special Purposes

1. Individual students can work in an area of need. For example, brighter students can extend their learning while slower students can focus on an area of deficiency.

2. Students are more motivated when they are studying something they have selected and in which they have a special interest.

3. Learning can be truly individualized, breaking the "lockstep" atmosphere of schools.

4. Individual students assume more responsibility for learning and the presenting of their projects or reports assists slower students to gain new insights into the study topic.

5. Students gain insights into "how" to learn.

6. Independent Study fosters self-teaching skills and attitudes.

7. All subject areas may be encompassed in this strategy.

8. A variety of exhibits can be used to demonstrate the results of a student's independent efforts.

Disadvantages or Limitations

1. The flexible schedules necessary to permit students and teachers to do true Independent Study may be lacking.

2. A shortage of related materials or other resources necessary to carry out the study may restrict independent work.

3. A lack of research skills on the part of the student and teacher may hinder completion of the project strategy.

4. Without proper background skills and training, a lack of initiative may become a severe problem in bringing the Independent Study project to a final conclusion.

5. The teacher must maintain a constant check of student progress where Independent Study programs are in operation.

6. Large amounts of time may be needed by the teacher to help each student individualize a program.

7. Evaluation is more difficult.

Guidelines for Maximum Utilization

1. Do not permit too many students to work on the same type of project. Often one student will do the major portion of the work and all will receive the same amount of credit in the final evaluation.

2. Take sufficient time at the beginning to help each student clarify the area of study. The student must have a clear understanding of the direction and limits of the study to be undertaken.

Clearly specified objectives should be stated at the outset of the project.

3. Determine the availability of resources before beginning this strategy.

4. Allow sufficient time to complete the project, but do not allow the project to continue endlessly (deadlines are usually beneficial).

5. Do not permit students to embark on studies which are not appropriate to class instruction. Students may be permitted to suggest areas of study, but you must have final approval to insure the appropriateness of the study.

6. It may be necessary to check progress at periodic intervals to review the individual's efforts and to provide additional guidance toward culmination of the project.

7. Determine in advance how the project will be presented for final evaluation. Criteria to determine the value of the project or the final grade evaluation should be established prior to the approval of an Independent Study proposal.

8. Permitting the students to share the results of their study with the rest of the class can add a dimension to the activity.

9. Make arrangements for alternate activities for those students who finish their project(s) earlier than anticipated.

Example

Hal Lockett, a high school history teacher, was having difficulty motivating one of his students in world history. In his evening graduate course in educational psychology he broached the subject to the professor, Dr. Whizz, a local school psychologist and adjunct instructor at the university.

"So," Dr. Whizz began, "you've tried the praise, the threats, the 'let me be your friend' approaches, and nothing happened?"

"No," Harold replied, "he just slumps in his seat, scowls, and mutters, 'What good is this stuff anyway?'"

"What does interest him?" Whizz queried.

"I don't know," Hal responded, "unless it's automobiles. He's always drawing cars, or reading auto magazines or shooting the bull with a guy next to him about engines, tune-ups, or racing slicks."

Dr. Whizz paced the front of the room for a few seconds. He suddenly stopped and looked straight at Hal. "Hal, what's going to happen to this fellow if you can't get him motivated in history?"

"Why, he'll get an F the way he's going."

"Exactly," exclaimed Whizz, "and that's why you have nothing to lose by catering to his interest, do you?"

Startled, Hal sat up straight. "What do you mean?"

"Look, Hal, do you really care how the boy learns history? I mean does he have to learn it your way or not at all?"

"Why, I don't care. I'd just be tickled to see him getting interested in the course. He's really got too much potential to flunk out of school."

"Good," the instructor responded, "so why not let him learn his world history by following the history of transportation from ancient times up to the modern automobile?"

"But," Hal questioned, "what about the curriculum guide? It doesn't allow for such an approach."

Dr. Whizz removed his glasses, his eyes glowing with intensity. "Hal, you and the curriculum guide are in existence to serve the learner, but curriculum guides are constructed to serve the majority of students. They will never meet the needs of every student. The teacher must maintain discretionary freedom in utilizing such guides—tailoring them to suit particular differences in students, whether those differences be class-wide or individual. You are hired to teach history successfully. If you pursue this student with the curriculum guide he will fail, and so will you. If you feel insecure, go to your principal and explain why and how you wish to set up an independent study with this boy. I'm sure he will buy the idea."

"OK," Hal responded, "how do I go about setting up an independent study?"

"First of all you locate the resources necessary for the project. Check libraries (by phone to save time), including school, public, and county libraries. Check not only for books, but also magazine articles, films, filmstrips, pamphlets, and reference works. This insures that the necessary resources are available. This is all done prior to springing the idea on the student. When you present him with the new approach, you want to know already what kind of structure you wish him to follow. Now this doesn't mean he cannot have input into the particular areas of concentration—encourage it—but *you* are the teacher. You establish the structure. This means you set the deadlines, and types of reporting (book reports, readings, projects, oral reports, etc.), record-keeping, and evaluation schema. It is very important that before he begins, the student be fully aware of:

"1. The objectives you specifically wish him to accomplish;

2. How you wish him to go about fulfilling the objectives, i.e., book reports, term papers, projects, etc.; and,

3. How he will be evaluated.

"The other crucial factor is that you touch base with him *every day* as to his progress. At least ask him, 'How is it going?' or something to that effect. *And,* at least once a week, check the folder and/or physical evidence of progress. Praise, encourage, cajole him until he gets in the swing of things. What do you think, will it work?"

"Yes, it certainly seems worth trying. Transportation history should catch his interest if anything will."

"Well," Dr. Whizz smiled, "it should provide a good vehicle for motivating him."

The class groaned.

Summary

Independent Study requires the teacher to allow the student to become the teacher. The teacher becomes a "guide-on-the-side" as opposed to a "sage-on-the-stage." This is a job of equal importance, but requires different functions: the teacher is an explainer of direction rather than a lecturer, an encourager rather than a demander, and a clarifier rather than a seeing-eye dog. It is not a time for rest and relaxation. If anything, the teacher must be more vigilant and more available for help than ever. Constant assessment of progress, conferring with the learner and viewing his/her work, is extremely important. It is an exhibition of concern—the greatest motivator one human can offer another.

Questions to Promote Discussion

1. One of the authors of this book feels the biggest weakness of our schools is not preparing students to learn "how" to learn. Do you agree or not? Why?

2. What do you consider to be the major limitation to using Independent Study in the classroom? What do you recommend to overcome that limitation?

3. What specific skills and attitudes do you think a student might develop through Independent Study that would not be learned in a "lockstep" classroom?

4. In using the Independent Study strategy, the teacher functions in a non-traditional manner. What are some teacher behaviors which must be adopted to use Independent Study? Would you be comfortable with those behaviors? Why or why not?

INDIVIDUALIZED LEARNING

Definition and Description

Individualized Learning is a broad, almost philosophical approach to the teaching-learning process. It involves an assessment of student needs and interests, a tailoring of subject matter and teaching strategies to meet those needs and interests, and constant monitoring and guidance of student progress. A teacher using this approach would employ a number of strategies; the concept of Individualized Learning is too universal to be applicable as a specific strategy. This universality is one of the reasons why the approach is not as widespread as most people believe it should be. In this amorphous state it is as difficult to understand as the concepts of patriotism, truth, and brotherly love. As with these concepts, Individualized Learning is understandable only through its displayed components: resources such as *learning packets, independent study, contracting, student research, programmed instruction, interest centers, interview, projects, Socratic, case study* and *student tutorial* strategies.

Advantages or Special Purposes

1. Each student moves at his own pace through a level of subject matter (matched with his assessed abilities), using a teaching/learning strategy selected to promote optimal progress.

2. Students are not floundering in material beyond their grasp or bored by material too easy for them.

3. Students are not penalized for being out of school for illness or family matters. Upon return each student can pick up at the point where he/she was temporarily halted.

4. Students are not in false competition with peers. They are only in competition with themselves.

5. Retention of learning is improved (over non-individualized instruction).

6. The instructor is truly a facilitating teacher wisely selecting a learning program to meet an individual's needs. The teacher observes daily activity and assists and/or adjusts programs as required.

7. The teacher has more opportunity to pinpoint and assist in solving individual student problems.

8. Many discipline problems arising from boredom and frustration are eliminated.

9. Evaluation takes the form of reporting actual individual accomplishments rather than the nebulous ABCDF grading system.

10. Students learn to take more responsibility for their own instructional activities.

11. Students have the opportunity to see their personal progress and tend to extend their knowledge rather than stopping at minimal levels of accomplishment.

Disadvantages or Limitations

1. Time and effort must be expended in developing materials and matching strategies to a given student.

2. Pre-assessment of student academic status takes time and special skill.

3. Students must be taught to handle individualized learning situations—a time-consuming activity.

4. Record-keeping can be lengthy and involved.

5. In the beginning individualized learning takes more teacher monitoring time.

6. Parents and administrators may be disturbed by the absence of letter grades.

7. The classroom physical structure and the classroom furniture may be limiting.

8. There is more movement and "noise" in an individualized classroom.

9. Appropriate resource materials may simply be unavailable.

10. Students may tend to work in competition with classmates rather than accept the challenge of self-improvement.

11. The teacher must be prepared to initiate new and continuing projects and study topics for those who learn and/or complete their work in shorter periods of time.

Guidelines for Maximum Utilization

Guidelines under each component strategy required should be consulted for specifics, but a few general helpful hints are in order.

1. Be prepared to gradually direct students away from the traditional to the individualized classroom. This will entail a great deal of structure at first until students become self-motivating and responsible.

2. Parents and pertinent administrators should be consulted for approval and kept informed prior to and during the program.

3. Careful records of individual accomplishments need to be kept, noting each student's daily progress.

4. Pre-assessment is an integral part of individualized learning. Different methods are plentiful, depending on the types of information required:

A. If physical health information is needed, consider the school nurse, cumulative records, parents, dialogue with the student, and your own observations.

B. If special learning disability information is needed you can rely on diagnostic tests, medical records, and conferences with the doctor, school psychologist, and parents.

C. To discover student interests and needs, use interest inventories, straightforward communication with the students, parent conferences and observation.

D. To learn about specific subject matter abilities, the use of pretests, conferences with the student's former teachers, achievement records, and observation will provide valuable information. Different subject matter may require different means of assessment.

5. Objectives should be clearly stated on paper and understood by the student.

6. Objectives and the time, material, and procedures necessary to achieve them should vary with each student's interest and capabilities.

7. Students should have some voice in selecting their objectives, materials, procedures, and time-span for completion. Ideally, they may eventually develop their own objectives and procedures.

8. Teacher and student must know at the outset what factors will be used for evaluation of the lesson material. A variety of evaluation techniques may be necessary in order to assure that each student is evaluated on his/her performance. Examples include: the quality of the work; grammatical quality; the number of biographical entries used; the ability of the student undertaking the individualized work; and the methods of presentation of learning results.

Summary

The processes used in Individualized Learning are not new. The good teacher has been aware of and has used them on a regular basis—but they have been directed at the entire class. Thus, the strategy has not been exploited to its fullest potential.

Although the strategy is time-consuming at the outset, the rewards tend to far exceed the energy expended. Students involved in individualized programs are encouraged to exceed minimal standards. They are further prompted to expand on lessons assigned to areas of their personal and intellectual interests. Consequently, learning becomes an exciting adventure and not a necessary obligation to complete the same daily activities that are performed in the typical classroom. It is truly a challenge to the intellectually inclined student but does not penalize those students who need to maintain a slower pace to accomplish the minimal requirements.

When coupled with other strategies such as *interest centers, student research,* and independent *laboratory* experiences, a program in Individualized Learning is a challenge to the student and a boon to the busy teacher.

Questions to Promote Discussion

1. Should individualized learning be listed as a separate strategy in a book on teaching strategies? Why or why not?

2. What is the major advantage of individualized learning?

3. What is the major disadvantage of individualized learning?

4. Which carries more weight, the advantage noted in response to Question #2 or the disadvantage noted in answer to Question #3? Why?

INTEREST CENTERS

Definition and Description

Establishing an Interest Centered Classroom (ICC) involves actual division of the physical space into stations of various academic areas. In an elementary classroom, for example, one might have a science center, a language arts center, a math center, a social science center, an art center, etc. An upper elementary or secondary classroom in biology might have a genetics center, a bacteriology center, an ecology center, an anatomy center, etc. Located in each center are abundant materials and equipment pertaining to that particular center's purpose.

In the "pure form" interest center, students spend as much time as they wish in any center. Variations are common in this strategy. Some teachers "contract" (see *contracting*) with students for objectives and time spent in each center, or require a certain amount of time per week in each interest center, or require a project in each interest center, etc.

Advantages or Special Purposes

1. Interest Centers provide for individualized learning within constraints of subject matter requirements.

2. Interest Centers allow students to devote more time to the subjects which interest them personally.

3. The teacher is free to move about from center to center assisting students.

4. Students have the opportunity to bring in their own materials with which to work.

5. Resource people in each interest area can be brought in easily to work with a small group of students.

6. Students are more responsible for their own learning activities.

7. The use of student tutors may work well in this strategy.

8. Where physical constraints limit the number of centers, a single center can be designated for a topical study and changed later to meet the next area or unit of study.

Disadvantages or Limitations

1. The physical arrangement of effective Interest Centers almost necessitates the replacement of individual student desks with tables and chairs and/or carpeting.

2. The need for varied materials in each center may be a constraint.

3. A great deal of preparation of environment, materials, *and* students is required.

4. Record-keeping of student achievement is difficult.

5. Students may be lacking in self-motivation—especially if they have not had prior independent work.

6. The teacher needs a good command of all subject matter.

7. The self-motivating, interest-based student behavior may not thrill administrators and parents as much as it does the students. Students make "noise" and move about more in an interest-centered class.

8. If students leave an interest-based class/year for a non-interest-based class/year there may be a problem with their re-adjustment.

Guidelines for Maximum Utilization

1. You must secure an abundance of materials and some
   equipment pertinent to each center well in advance of the
   beginning of the year. This involves a lot of time, and some
   begging or borrowing from local businesses, individuals,
   hospitals, etc. (unless you have no budget problems). The type
   and quantity of materials depend on the objectives for each
   center. It is amazing how much you can gain by donation if you
   just ask.

2. Resource people are a valuable asset to an interest-based
   classroom. Likewise, they must be lined up and informed as to
   what is expected of them ahead of time. Often it is possible to
   have a resource person come in regularly to work with a small
   group in a certain field. Just as with materials, it is amazing how
   many experts are pleased to donate their time and energy to
   work with students. Do not fail to utilize some students' parents
   and acquaintances as valuable resources.

3. Administration and parents should be kept informed and/or
   consulted during the planning and program operation.

4. If students are not acquainted with self-motivating classrooms, it
   will be essential to have a "weaning period" during which they
   are structured into their activities (perhaps by contracting)
   rather closely at first. As individual students gain more
   confidence and responsibility they can begin structuring their
   own learning activities.

5. Each student should have a folder kept in a central file where
   he logs his activities and achievements. (If contracts are utilized,
   they should also be kept in the folder for both your and the
   students' referral.) Care should be taken that accurate and
   detailed records are kept; otherwise, evaluation becomes
   impossible.

6. Another possibility for evaluation is to require each student to
   exhibit some level of individual proficiency on small quizzes or
   written exercises.

7. Depending on how structured the situation is, students can be encouraged to bring their own materials and resource people (after they're cleared by the teacher).

8. Many other strategies can operate effectively within the interest-centered classroom—*projects, independent study, research, student tutorial, field trips, learning packets,* etc. As an example, the *behavior modification* strategy can be utilized by setting up an Interest Center of games. Students can go there for free time after completing a specified amount of academic work.

Summary

Interest Center teaching can be a terrific blessing. It individualizes learning, makes students more responsible for their own time (allows them to spend more time where needed), encourages communication with the "outside world," and eliminates many motivational problems. It also makes progress reporting easier and meaningful, as parents can be shown the student's file on what he/she has actually accomplished rather than just a letter grade.

A major objection to this type of classroom operation is the procurement of materials and equipment; this is, in actuality, a display of non-initiative and non-imagination on the part of the objector. A good creative teacher can procure almost anything for little or no cost (even a rocket was acquired by one teacher!) if proper communication is established. Federal, state and local agencies have literally tons of material and equipment that can be donated, or at least borrowed. Many agencies, such as the State Department of Natural Resources, large industry, law enforcement, etc., have people on their staff whose main function is to perform public relations work. There is a wealth of knowledge and skill in one of our most ignored resources—the retired professional. Hospital personnel, veterinarians and engineers are usually very willing to visit classrooms. The list goes on and on.

With proper introduction and monitoring the teacher may find that Interest-Centered teaching provides the valuable organizational assistance for which he or she has been searching.

Questions to Promote Discussion

1. Would you expect the students at the grade level which you anticipate teaching to be in favor of using Interest Centers? Why or why not?

2. Assuming you had the materials and space, what do you think the major obstacle to using Interest Centers would be? Why?

3. What steps could you take to overcome this obstacle?

4. What would you predict to be the "future" of the use of Interest Centers? Why?

INTERVIEW

Definition and Description

The Interview is basically a data-gathering technique using pre-planned questions to determine the feelings and attitudes of an individual, a specific group, the school, or the community on an issue of high interest. It is closely related to the survey in that both seek to develop data—one by oral questioning and the other through written response.

The Interview is especially helpful in practicing a one-on-one situation such as a guidance counselor-student Interview or a student-citizen Interview on a pre-established question or problem. It may be used in random sampling of a few people to establish a trend (similar to Gallup or Harris Polls) or in seeking opinions from high public officials and other select individuals.

An Interview is performed in a systematic fashion within a few simple guidelines:

1. Outline the general plan.

2. Establish rapport with the respondent.

3. State the issue, question or problem.

4. Elicit a response to the issue, question or problem.

5. Record the data.

6. Close the Interview.

7. Evaluate and report findings.

Advantages or Special Purposes

1. Interviews encourage students to plan and think in a systematic fashion.

2. This is an excellent method for collecting data from individuals and groups.

3. It is especially useful in collection of information related to community attitudes and personal opinions.

4. Persons interviewed generally have a high degree of interest and a desire to express their personal opinion.

5. Through the use of this strategy, information on an issue or problem can be collected quickly.

6. Interviewing helps develop rapport between the school and the community.

7. It can be used as an individual or total class project.

8. If well planned, it helps bring the pupil face-to-face with community realities.

Disadvantages or Limitations

1. The teacher must spend a substantial amount of time helping students develop questioning techniques.

2. Interviewing requires a coordinated effort of all involved, and this can disrupt school or administrative routines.

3. A poorly planned Interview can result in erroneous learning and impaired public relations.

4. Students tend to take sides on an issue rather than remain neutral.

5. The data are often difficult to interpret and report.

6. The class may not be of sufficient maturity to face the obligations required in performing Interviews, especially when meeting older members of the community.

7. Interviews tend to elicit personal opinions and may not be factual or usable in the final reports.

Guidelines for Maximum Utilization

1. Plan Interviews well in advance and rehearse techniques prior to actual Interview situations.

2. Be selective in choosing questions and issues. The issue should be relevant and interesting, the questions clear and designed to gather the necessary type and amount of data.

3. Develop specific questions. (Note: the teacher may want to review the strategy of *questioning* at this point.)

4. The questions should be free of bias.

5. Before initiating this strategy, secure administrative approval.

6. Students should avoid taking sides of an issue (until all data are in and analyzed).

7. Encourage students to be pleasant, courteous and tactful during Interviews.

8. During the Interview take notes in brief written form, or, if using a recorder, secure permission in advance to record the remarks.

9. Establish guidelines with which to evaluate results prior to actual Interviews.

10. Be prepared to respond to the interviewee's return questions.

Summary

Crucial to the success of the Interview strategy is preparation in: (1) knowing the background of the interviewee; (2) knowing the information desired from the Interview; and, (3) knowing what questions need to be asked to accumulate that information.

An important facet of interviewing is the attitude of the person conducting the Interview. A successful interviewer rivets his/her attention to the person being interviewed, as if the rest of the world has disappeared. That person is the most important in the world—his/her words are pearls of wisdom, drops of pure nectar, and if not attended to will be lost forever. (In actuality, this may be more truth than poetry, and not a bad attitude for students to develop.) The interviewer, in effect, creates a vacuum (a dismissal of his own identity) which draws out information from the subject.

Interview is a useful strategy. It teaches students to gather information in a logical and respectful fashion from a most valuable temporary resource—another human being. This has been the basis of recent usage to document "living history" lessons.

Questions to Promote Discussion

1. Name a project in which students could serve as interviewers.

2. What would be the major advantage for students conducting Interviews in this subject?

3. Why is student interviewing not often used by teachers?

4. Should Interviewing be used more often? Why or why not?

LABORATORY

Definition and Description

The *Dictionary of Education* defines the Laboratory strategy as:

> the instructional procedure by which the cause, effect, nature or property of any phenomenon, whether social, psychological or physical, is determined by actual experience or experiment under controlled conditions.

In its "pure" form, Laboratory is conceived to be a sterile, well equipped room with white-coated technicians carrying out a variety of experiments and activities. Today, Laboratory is defined as the place where an individual or group study some phenomenon, subject, lesson, etc. It could be a reading lab, outdoor education center, science facility, or an ordinary classroom.

In simple terms, Laboratory is a supervised learning activity carried out by the student studying a particular subject involving practical application of theory through observation, experimentation, and research.

Advantages or Special Purposes

1. Students can capitalize on their own interests.

2. The teacher is free to offer individual assistance and instruction to those students needing special attention.

3. The activity may be carried out by individual students or in small groups.

4. Instruction may be done through the use of self-instructional materials, devices, or machines.

5. Laboratory is basically a problem-solving technique, usually of short duration.

6. This strategy helps students learn to generalize and to apply generalizations in new situations.

7. As a learning activity, it reinforces the discovery and inquiry approaches to learning.

8. Laboratory simulates actual scientific experiments including the formulation of hypotheses, testing the hypotheses, recording and reporting the findings.

9. Students increase their ability to do the tasks more effectively, more skillfully, and more independently.

10. It is an excellent motivational strategy.

11. Groups are provided the opportunity to share in the results and findings of individual projects.

Disadvantages or Limitations

1. The approved projects must be within the range of the students' abilities.

2. The maturity of the students may be insufficient to pursue long-range goals established.

3. Individual students may lack the motivation to work alone.

4. Some students develop a poor estimation of self-esteem if they experience slow progress or failure.

5. The Laboratory strategy may cause the teacher to supervise individuals to the exclusion of the group.

6. Costs may exceed the benefits.

7. Unless well organized, it can become wasted time and effort on the part of all concerned.

8. Learning may become mechanical and passive.

9. This method is difficult to apply to all curricula.

10. It is difficult to develop projects so that all students have equally challenging activities and experiences.

11. The teacher faces problems because of the uneven starting and stopping points.

Guidelines for Maximum Utilization

1. The use of this strategy requires close planning and coordination between the teacher and the learner.

2. The approval of projects must be within the capability of the student, teacher and academic situation.

3. It requires facilities with flexibility.

4. Care must be taken to see that appropriate materials and supplies are available.

5. The teacher must select appropriate criteria in advance for the final evaluation of the students' projects.

6. Arrange approval by the administration for questionable projects.

7. Relate the results to previously studied material.

8. Establish time limits for completion of Laboratory work.

9. Don't allow the project to become busy work.

10. Plan alternative activities for those who finish their laboratory work earlier than anticipated.

11. Students should maintain a lab notebook or log of accomplishments.

Summary

If Laboratory experiences are not always limited to "cookbook experiments" (Place a drop of iodine on the bread. What color does the bread become? _____ What does this mean? _____), they can give students the opportunity to *do* learning as opposed to reading about other peoples' learning. Retention and interest increase with greater frequency and, perhaps, even creative thought is exercised.

Success is determined mostly by teacher preparation and direction appropriate to the learner's ability. *Some* structure is definitely necessary if predictable results are desired. It is important to remember that Laboratory learning teaches process as well as production.

Questions to Promote Discussion

1. What advantage to learning does the Laboratory approach offer that no other approach offers? Explain.

2. In your estimation, what is the most glaring inadequacy of the Laboratory strategy? Explain why.

3. Is there any way to compensate for the inadequacy noted in answer to Question #2? Why, or why not?

LEARNING PACKETS

Definition and Description

The Unipac, Lappak, Learn-a-pac, and others are sets of self-contained learning materials assembled for the purpose of teaching a single concept or idea. They are generally structured for individual use and are most effectively used in schools with flexible curricula, although they are not limited to these settings. The Learning Packet may be an excellent means of initiating *individualized learning*.

The unit package consists of a series of sequential learning activities leading to the achievement of desired outcomes (stated in behavioral terms) by the learners. Components of the Learning Packets may include:

-Teacher directions
-Student instructions
-Pre-test
-Major and sub-concepts
-Behavioral objectives
-Assorted strategies and content
-Student self-assessment
-Post-test
-Research activities
-Independent resource and study materials

The Learning Packet is designed to help students achieve at their own best learning rate. The teacher is a resource person available to offer assistance as the student pursues the learning content of the instructional package.

Because the unit is designed for individual use, a series of units may be developed on a single topic area. Each may be of increasing difficulty, requiring the learner to develop new skills, techniques and greater knowledge.

Advantages or Special Purposes

1. Students are able to pursue special interest areas yet still work within the confines of the total curriculum.

2. Learning takes place in a sequential order.

3. All concepts are stated in behavioral (measurable) terms.

4. Materials in Learning Packets can be developed for all levels of learning.

5. Any discipline can be the subject of Learning Packets.

6. Learning Packets may be exchanged both within the school and with other schools.

7. The Learning Packet is well planned from start to finish.

8. Using the pre-test and post-test, the teacher is able immediately to evaluate the amount of learning that has taken place.

9. Teachers are placed in the role of facilitators of learning rather than directors of learning.

10. Students gain broader insight into learning through the use of varied materials and activities and by doing research in their special interest areas.

Disadvantages or Limitations

1. Unit packets are time consuming to develop.

2. They are often misused as testing devices rather than learning units.

3. The Learning Packet requires an abundance of resource materials in order to complete the total project.

4. Teachers tend to treat unit packages as isolated projects rather than as part of the total curriculum.

5. Students may tend to get bored with lengthy learning units.

6. Students may not have the maturity to work independently.

Guidelines for Maximum Utilization

1. Take time to understand thoroughly how to develop and use Learning Packets.

2. Take the time to work through the unit prior to classroom use, to be sure it is complete and accurate.

3. Plan well in advance to see that all necessary materials and resources are available.

4. Follow the directions for teachers within the Learning Packet.

5. Establish a definite time period for completion of the unit of learning.

6. Confer with each student as he or she progresses, to clarify activities and to provide continuous evaluation.

7. Relate the Learning Packet to the curriculum. (Do not allow it to become isolated from learning goals.)

8. Check to assure yourself that the school organization has the required flexibility to pursue this type of learning activity.

Summary

If a teacher ever desired to have learning materials pre-packaged, those prayers have been answered. The Learning Packet is complete from beginning to end except for the inclusion of a motivation pill for the student. This job is left up to the teacher, as always. "Facilitation" by the teacher means proper direction and explanation before the student begins the unit, encouragement and guidance during involvement, and proper supervision of evaluation and unit conclusion. Encouragement and positive reinforcement are important to the success of this strategy since only a minority of public school age students is totally self-motivating in independent work.

Above all, the teacher must have a thorough understanding of each Learning Packet. Since there are specific instructions for the teacher, they should be adhered to strictly.

Questions to Promote Discussion

1. Which do you feel to be the wiser course of action: buying commercially prepared learning packets or developing your own? Why?

2. If you were to consider using learning packets, what do you believe would be the major problem to face? Why?

3. What steps would you take to overcome the problem elicited in the preceding question?

4. What do you consider to be the unique feature of using Learning Packets? Why?

THE LECTURE

Definition and Description

The Lecture is the traditional method of teaching wherein the lecturer transmits information in an autocratic fashion to passive student listeners. In the pure form, students have no opportunity to ask questions or offer comments during the Lecture.

Advantages or Special Purposes

1. The Lecture is most helpful in introducing a new topic of study or presenting certain background material that students need for preparation of further study.

2. Lecture permits a large audience to receive succinct information quickly about aspects of materials that will increase their understanding of what lies ahead.

3. Lecture provides students with an organized perspective of the content to be considered.

4. Lecture provides practice for the students in learning to develop notetaking skills.

5. The Lecture provides the teacher with a sense of "security" since no surprising information will be introduced into the session.

Disadvantages or Limitations

1. Lengthy or overly frequent lectures can easily lead to boredom.

2. The lecturer has difficulty in assessing impact on the audience and whether student needs and interests are being met.

3. Individuals in the group are not permitted to ask questions, thus eliminating feedback and leading to miscommunication.

4. Detailed and factual information is difficult to "communicate" or "relate" in such a setting.

5. Affective (attitudes) and psycho-motor learning seldom occur as the result of a Lecture.

6. Higher level cognitive learning is seldom achieved by students since they do not actively work with the information being considered.

Guidelines for Maximum Utilization

1. Know the overall goals and specific objectives while planning the Lecture.

2. Know the audience. What are their specific needs and interests? Goals should then mesh with these needs and interests in order to eliminate boredom and to help students grow.

3. The Lecture should be well organized so that the logic is as "perceivable" as possible. This includes planning of methodology, utilization of equipment, demonstration materials, handouts, etc.

4. Vary the Lecture by using interest-arousing aids such as pictures, models and other visuals. The chalkboard serves as a useful tool for outlining or emphasizing important points.

5. Avoid monotonous-type lecturing by varying voice stress and intensity. Try to stir students' imaginations by painting with vivid word pictures.

6. Avoid "pure" Lecture by utilizing questions during the Lecture. Two kinds of questions may be used: (1) the kind you ask—pause—and answer yourself (rhetorical), and (2) the kind you expect students to answer. Both are attention-getters and the second has the added benefit of requiring mental answer-search on the part of the students as well as providing a feedback mechanism to enable the lecturer to measure audience absorption.

7. Always allow ample opportunity for questions to come from the students.

8. Watch the audience. Their actions (attentiveness) will reveal the effectiveness of the lecture.

9. After the Lecture, attempt to break into buzz sessions or other small groups to develop clarification of the materials discussed. The lecturer should circulate from group to group.

10. Revise Lecture approach on the basis of feedback (6, 7, and 8 above).

Summary

Lecture: the oldest form of teaching, and one of the most ineffective—ineffective because it is overused, abused, and misused. Lectures should be short, sweet, and to the point—when they are necessary at all. Generally speaking, Lectures are ineffective because they place the learner in a very passive posture. This lack of activity is extremely conducive to boredom and daydreaming, and it sometimes spawns discipline problems. Lecture assumes that the lecturer knows all and the "lecturee" is ignorant, and this automatically turns off some listeners. The degree to which this happens is determined to some extent by the attitude of the lecturer while making the presentation.

Lecture is most effective in clarifying or demonstrating a procedure or skill.

Questions to Promote Discussion

1. For years many educators and students have been extremely critical of the overuse of Lectures. However, the Lecture approach is still overused. Why?

2. What is the chief limitation of the Lecture? Why?

3. What should the teacher do to overcome this limitation?

MASTERY LEARNING

Definition and Description

Mastery Learning is used by many persons to mean a variety of things. It is not new in education, but has come back into vogue recently. The basis for this new interest stems from D. J. Muellar's "mastery learning instructional model." The model includes the following basic components:

1. Formal development of a comprehensive set of cognitive objectives.

2. Instruction, using a variety of teaching methods.

3. Frequent evaluation, both formal and diagnostic.

4. Corrective and/or remedial instruction.

5. Criterion-referenced summative evaluation (a review by testing over the entire process).

The objectives are first clearly specified for the lesson or unit to be learned. This is followed by the traditional instructional methods used in any classroom. After instruction, all students are tested for mastery of the specific objectives. Those students exhibiting deficiencies are given additional instruction and time to master the objectives of the lesson. The important aspect of Mastery Learning is that a student must demonstrate competency before moving to the next learning segment.

Advantages or Special Purposes

1. The strategy can be used in any subject area.

2. Objectives are clearly listed prior to beginning the lesson.

3. The class works on the lesson as a group, with the teacher noting individual needs for special help at a later time.

4. The individual students do not feel singled out if they learn at a slower rate than their peers.

5. Specific needs of individuals are succinctly defined and treated without delay or lag time.

6. The strategy works equally well in corrective or remedial situations.

7. Mastery of initial and early units forms the basis for the next unit.

8. It tends to build confidence in the learner with each unit mastered.

9. Although the strategy is time consuming, the results are extremely satisfying when properly executed to a conclusion.

Disadvantages or Limitations

1. The programs used must be flexible enough to accommodate the wide disparity of abilities within the classroom.

2. Flexibility for meeting diverse cultural backgrounds is necessary and difficult to achieve in some subject areas.

3. Teachers often lack the necessary expertise to carry out programs of Mastery Learning.

4. The curriculum (subject) objectives must be clearly specified—often a difficult and time-consuming task.

5. The strategy can be time consuming if student ability and achievement ranges are extremely wide.

6. Evaluation and follow-up instruction for remediation and corrective measures require explicit planning.

7. Paper work, record keeping and follow-up activities call for assistance from teacher aides or peer tutors.

8. Mastery Learning works best in subjects requiring cognitive skills in which memorization is important.

Guidelines for Maximum Utilization

1. Develop clear, sequential cognitive objectives for the specific lesson and unit before beginning instruction.

2. Prepare sufficient activity sheets, high-interest reading materials, puzzles, games and other enrichment activities in advance to meet the needs of individuals who complete a mastery lesson earlier than anticipated.

3. Give clear directions and, preferably, an example of procedure to students before beginning the lesson. Evaluative criteria should also be made quite clear in advance.

4. Prepare to enter the Mastery Learning strategy by experimenting with a simple lesson before attempting more complex ones.

5. Formative tests must be prepared in advance for use at the end of a lesson or unit.

6. Ditto masters of remedial and diagnostic materials should be prepared prior to the lesson for immediate follow-up activities with those having difficulty.

Summary

For those who are into "Accountability" (whether by choice or chance) Mastery Learning provides a vehicular strategy. A student may not take the next learning step in the sequence until he/she has mastered the lower level.

Theoretically it sounds wonderful to say "guaranteed learning," but the opposite side of the coin is a regimented and boring approach to learning. Only periodic use of this strategy is recommended. The problem with this approach is now being discovered by some teachers who are using Mastery Learning Total Curriculum Kits in kindergarten classrooms. The mastery chart on the wall looks efficient with its little boxes behind each child's name, but behavior problems begin to develop rapidly when curriculum demands that students approach learning as a series of hurdles.

Study the processes, use it if it conforms to your needs, but use it wisely and correctly.

Questions to Promote Discussion

1. What are the pros and cons of Mastery Learning academically? Psychologically?

2. How does Mastery Learning promote "accountability"?

3. What would a comprehensive set of cognitive objectives look like in your teaching field?

4. What instructional strategies would you most favor using in conjunction with Mastery Learning? Why?

OBSERVATION

Definition and Description

Observation is probably more of a teacher skill than a strategy. However, its importance is so crucial to effective use of other strategies and it is so intricately intertwined with all of them that it becomes almost imperative to treat it as a "pure form" strategy.

An "observer" is usually thought of as an unobtrusive person sitting in the corner passively watching students. It is a rare teacher who has the luxurious opportunity to observe his own students perform. Therefore, we shall define Observation as "astute perception by the teacher of multi-faceted student behavior, attitudes, and learning problems while in the midst of a dynamic classroom situation." In other words, the teacher should be aware of "what's happening." To be constantly cognizant of what is transpiring throughout the class is not an easy task. It is especially difficult for those teachers who are in the habit of seeing "the group" rather than the individuals who compose the group. It is of utmost importance to be "omnisciently observant," as this is the major and only *immediate* way to learn of student reactions to the general environment and particular learning segments.

Advantages or Special Purposes

1. Through Observation much can be learned concerning student physiological problems (hearing, vision, speech, coordination, bodily defects, etc.) and needs (diet supplements, hygiene care, clothing, etc.).

2. Observation yields a great deal of information about the learner's socio-emotional development.

3. The data supplied by the two above practices are necessary for the teacher's precise observance of students' academic problems. For example, if the student is observed to be having an academic difficulty, does the cause lie in the student's physiological/socio-emotional realms or does it arise from teacher/subject matter areas (lack of student readiness, improper or unclear directions, irrelevant or uninteresting material or methods, etc.)?

4. Observation provides immediate information and feedback, whereas testing or diagnostics lessen the effect of problem-attention due to the time-delay. Many potential learning problems can be eliminated by prompt action, ultimately saving a great deal of energy and discomfort on the part of both teacher and student.

5. Keen observations eliminate many discipline problems before they occur.

6. The obvious interest displayed by the teacher leaves no doubt in the students' minds that the instructor is concerned about them. This provides for a mutually pleasant and positive learning environment and tends to increase growth in all domains.

7. As the teacher becomes increasingly aware of the effects of various strategies in different situations (and alters teaching approaches on the basis of that information) he becomes a constantly self-improving professional, always seeking a better way.

Disadvantages or Limitations

1. It is difficult to become a sharp observer. It requires determined practice at separating oneself into two people—a person "teaching" (demonstrating, lecturing, utilizing AV material, passing out papers, etc.) and a person "observing" (alert to physiological, socio-emotional, learning, and behavioral aspects).

2. It is difficult to be objective; we all tend to feel, "*I* am objective, but they are not." This usually false predisposition

prevents the teacher from examining his/her own observational objectivity. Therefore, Observation is often prejudicial and the results can be more harmful than helpful.

3. There is a tendency to "play favorites," to observe only children who are pleasing to watch.

4. There is a tendency to watch for only negative occurrences, thereby failing to notice and accentuate positive traits being exhibited.

5. The inclination is to be solely on the alert for particulars, which can lead to failure to sense the total classroom atmosphere.

Guidelines for Maximum Utilization

1. The teacher should plan on the necessary self-training in Observation skills. A daily skill goal should be established and carried out in all contacts with students. Some sample goals might be:

   1st day: Which students appear to pay attention? When?
   2nd day: Which students appear not to pay attention? When?
   3rd day: What habits (repeated behaviors) are exhibited by which students?
   4th day: Which students appear to have vision difficulty? Hearing problems?
   5th day: Who are the isolates? How do they behave differently?
   6th day: Which students attempt to monopolize your attention? What methods do they use?
   7th day: What physical handicaps are present?
   8th day: Which students like to tease? How? To whom do they direct their teasing?
   9th day: Who dominates discussions? When?
   10th day: Who appears to need peer approval? How do they go about it? When?
   11th day: What rewards work best with which students?
   12th day: What rewards work best with which students? (It takes *at least* two days.).

13th day: Which students cooperate with which other students?
When?
14th day: Which students cooperate with you? When?
15th day: Who are the silent leaders? When?
16th day: Who appears to have difficulty with which subject
matter (or particular part of the subject matter)?
17th day: Who asks questions? When? What kind?
18th day: Who appears to read with comprehension? When?
19th day: Who appears to read with comprehension? When?
20th day: Who appears to get emotionally upset? When?

And the list could go on and on. Practice at looking for particular traits or behaviors eventually sharpens the teacher's observation powers beyond belief. The teacher's eye becomes so discerning that a mountain of information can be compiled with a few glances around the classroom.

2. Observations should be as objective as possible. Until we have the ability to enter other peoples' minds to see actually why they do the things they do, we must restrict our descriptions to *observable behavior*. This eliminates such value-laden judgments as: "Bill was very 'bad' when he . . . "; "Martha has an 'annoying' habit of . . . "; and "Jane constantly has a 'harmful effect' on . . . " Such prejudicial statements, although seemingly correct to the observer, may be extremely inaccurate, and can only lead to distortion of the true situation. Once this happens, corrective behavior by the teacher stands an excellent chance of being irrelevant, and probably detrimental, to the learning environment and the people involved.

3. Only after one has carefully considered the evidence as to why certain student behavior is exhibited should one attempt to accentuate positive behavior and eliminate negative behavior through utilization of new learning strategies or positive disciplinary measures. (It is at this point that a program of *behavior modification* may be initiated.)

4. Never neglect your built-in "environmental thermostat." Despite looking for particular behaviors, you must constantly attune part of your observation powers to the classroom atmosphere. Is it conducive or detrimental to learning? Is it

time to do something else—take a break, go on a field trip, have free time, or change subject matter?

Summary

Observation is perception. Accurate perception is invaluable to the proficient teacher. It might be the fundamental strategy underlying effective use of all other strategies. How else is a teacher to judge when and how to plug in different strategies if he/she is not gaining accurate input on student needs and desires?

Most of us are fairly poor observers. Although the teacher is supposed to reinforce students towards progress, who motivates the teacher to improve? Usually not principals or paychecks. It is purely on the teacher's shoulders to be mature and professional enough to take a step and enjoy the feeling of "doing better." Observation, if practiced, can be one of the most rewarding steps ever taken.

Questions to Promote Discussion

1. In your opinion, should "Observation" be included in a book of teaching strategies? Why or why not?

2. What is the major disadvantage or limitation of Observation? Explain.

3. How would a teacher overcome the problem cited in answer to Question #2?

4. What can Observation, as described, most contribute to the teacher? Is that important? Explain.

PROBLEM-SOLVING

Definition and Description

The name "problem-solving" is assigned to learning approaches based upon the scientific method of inquiry. These approaches are built upon John Dewey's five steps of general Problem-Solving: (1) defining the problem, (2) formulating tentative hypotheses, (3) collecting, evaluating, organizing, and interpreting data, (4) reaching conclusions, and (5) testing those conclusions. For example, a social studies class might become concerned about what will happen in Cuba when Castro dies. The problem then becomes: what happens to the dictatorship when a dictator dies?

The class members discuss various alternatives and then finally state their hypothesis: When a dictator dies, the dictatorship ends. Next, they would collect, evaluate, organize and interpret data. They would study dictators throughout history and what happened to the dictatorship upon the death of each dictator. The data might either support or deny the hypothesis.

Next a conclusion would be reached regarding what generally has happened to the dictatorship when the dictator dies. The degree to which the hypothesis is supported or denied by the evidence determines the conclusion. The conclusion would then be applied to Castro and a prediction could be made. (Time would enable the prediction to be tested.)

Advantages or Special Purposes

1. Because the student has been actively involved, comprehension and retention should be of longer duration.

2. Problem-Solving provides the student with a model to apply to problems that may be faced in the future.

3. Problem-Solving involves cognitive (including higher levels) and affective learning.

4. Problem-Solving develops responsibility in the learner.

5. Interest in learning and motivation are increased with the use of Problem-Solving.

6. Students utilize materials and resources other than a single textbook.

7. Students learn how to think independently in reaching conclusions.

8. Problem-Solving provides the opportunity for students to learn from failure without severe hardships.

9. The student learns to accept the opinions of others.

Disadvantages or Limitations

1. Materials and resources needed for Problem-Solving often are not available to the students.

2. Problem-Solving can be time consuming.

3. Students may tend to become negative in outlook in that the only worthwhile area of study is a "problem."

4. Students are often too immature to really recognize problems of social significance.

5. The teacher must be very well prepared in the discipline.

6. The issues that are controversial in nature may create problems with administrators, parents or community groups.

7. Evaluation of learning is difficult.

Guidelines for Maximum Utilization

1. Expose the student to a number of similar problems.

2. The problems presented must fit the maturation and skill levels of the student.

3. The student must see the problem as being important.

4. Assist pupils in defining and delimiting the problem to be studied.

5. Check for sufficient resources and materials to be available for student use.

6. Provide guidance and direction when necessary, taking care not to overdo it.

7. Help students establish criteria with which to make appropriate evaluations.

Summary

Problem-Solving moves the mind to some of its highest cognitive functions: analyzing, generalizing, and synthesizing. This alone justifies it as one of the most valuable of all strategies. Magnifying the value is accomplished if the problems to be solved are relevant and interesting to the students. It is impossible to over-estimate the importance of topic selection and preparation/planning. The teacher would be wise to assess, by oral or written survey, the interests of pupils prior to topic selection. Ms. Rosemary Daniell, a poet-in-residence on Lookout Mountain, wanted to find out the elementary children's real interests before selecting poetry topics. She found that the children were fascinated with three things: mainly death, dreams, and God. All of these were, of course, not in the school curriculum or in her thought list. The shift to these topics was very rewarding. The children could not write enough poetry for Ms. Daniell, and motivation was no problem. The survey certainly was worth the little time and effort required.

An added benefit in utilizing this strategy is that students become adept at digging up information and cross-checking its validity with other resources. Critical thinking is a too infrequent exercise for most students and the Problem-Solving strategy is part of the solution of this dilemma.

Questions to Promote Discussion

1. Choose a problem and describe how the teacher could use the Problem-Solving approach in the classroom.

2. What do you consider to be the major advantage of the Problem-Solving approach? Why?

3. What do you consider to be the chief limitation of the Problem-Solving approach? Why?

4. How would you overcome the problem identified in response to Question #3?

PROGRAMMED LEARNING (INSTRUCTION)

Definition and Description

The *Dictionary of Education* describes Programmed Instruction as:

> instruction utilizing a workbook, textbook, or mechanical and/or electronic device programmed to help pupils attain a specific level of performance by (a) providing instruction in small steps, (b) asking one or more questions about each step in the instruction and providing instant knowledge of whether each answer is right or wrong, and (c) enabling pupils to progress at their own pace, either individually through self-pacing or as a team through group-pacing.

The psychological principles of Programmed Instruction are stimulus, response, and reinforcement. The small steps (frames) are designed in sequential arrangements and detail so that the student will generally make correct responses. These responses are then reinforced.

Auto-instruction and automated teaching are synonyms for Programmed Instruction. Machine teaching, often erroneously termed Programmed Instruction, is only one type of Programmed Instruction.

One method of programming is variously termed linear, fixed-sequence, straight-line, or extrinsic. In such an approach, the units of content are designed in small sequential steps which must be completed in the pre-arranged order.

The other basic method of programming is called nonlinear, branching, or intrinsic. In this approach, the student responds to a

presented step, or frame. The next frame the student faces depends
upon his response. If correct, the student goes on to a new exercise.
If incorrect, the student may be referred to remedial exercises.

In the following sample program, note the linear quality of the
program.

Sentence to Be Completed	Word to Be Supplied
1. The important parts of a flashlight are the battery and the bulb. When we "turn on" a flashlight, we close a switch which connects the battery with the _____.	bulb
2. When we turn on a flashlight, an electric current flows through the fine wire in the _____ and causes it to grow hot.	bulb
3. When the hot wire glows brightly, we say that it gives off or sends out heat and _____.	light
4. The fine wire in the bulb is called a filament. The bulb "lights up" when the filament is heated by the passage of a(n) _____ current.	electric
5. When a weak battery produces little current, the fine wire, or _____, does not get very hot.	filament
6. A filament which is *less* hot sends off or gives off _____ light.	less
7. "Emit" means "send out." The amount of light sent out, or "emitted," by a filament depends on how _____ the filament is.	hot

Source: B. F. Skinner, "Teaching Machines," *Science*, Vol. 128 (October 24, 1958), p. 973.

Advantages or Special Purposes

1. Programmed Instruction saves the teacher a considerable
amount of time.

2. The time saved can be applied to individuals or groups at either remedial or higher intellectual learning.

3. Programmed Instruction is effective for remedial teaching, drill and practice, as well as enrichment.

4. The learner is actively responding at all times to the program.

5. The student progresses at his/her own rate and level of achievement.

6. The success and reinforcement given the student provides motivation for the learner.

7. Research has demonstrated that students can learn effectively through programmed instruction.

8. Students can study programs on their own which are not part of the ordinary curriculum.

9. The student, through immediate feedback, is aware of the degree of progress being made.

Disadvantages or Limitations

1. Good programs are hard to identify and not all programs on the market are worth using.

2. Writing programs is a very difficult process which causes teachers generally to rely on commercial programs.

3. The kinds of materials and types of learning which can be programmed are limited. For example, the material must be that which contains a right answer.

4. Programmed Instruction is not very applicable to affective or psychomotor learning.

5. The cost of materials and/or machines can be prohibitive.

6. Some students complain that programs are dull, boring or repetitious.

7. Programmed Instruction for individual development does not fit the school's structure of time, semesters, credit hours, etc.

Guidelines for Maximum Utilization

1. Thoroughly study the objectives of the program to be sure they fit the objectives of the teacher.

2. Completely work through the program in order to check out its applicability and to better understand what the student will experience.

3. Use programmed materials to meet the individual needs of students.

4. Realize that any attempt to use programmed materials is somewhat experimental.

5. Begin utilizing programs for a unit of content, then evaluate the experience to decide upon further use.

6. Programmed Instruction is usually most effective when used periodically rather than all of the time.

7. Students can learn much by actually making their own programs. A side benefit of this is that excellently constructed ones can be used with future students.

Summary

For a time Programmed Learning was a rage. Total courses were taught with this strategy. The rage subsided and so did the utilization of Programmed Instruction. In a way, it's not surprising—this is the usual pattern in education; a new fad is overused to the point of negating its value. This is unfortunate. A course with Programmed Instruction as the sole method of learning can be devastatingly boring and tedious, but properly used on a once-in-a-while basis it can be fun and provides variety. It is especially useful in science and mathematics, and materials can be found or constructed for all learner levels, whether slow, average, or gifted.

Materials can be bought, teacher-made, student-made, or borrowed. They can be reused (if separate answer sheets are dittoed) year after year, and rarely need updating as they usually cover basic concepts (magnetism, Civil War, long division, etc.).

The biggest point in favor of Programmed Instruction is that it is another method in the arsenal of *individualized learning*, an overall strategy heartily endorsed by the authors.

Questions to Promote Discussion

1. There was a time when some people believed the teaching machine (utilizing programs) would replace the classroom teacher. This did not happen. What disadvantages or limitations of Programmed Instruction do you feel contributed to this? Why?

2. In what ways can Programmed Instruction be a real benefit to the student? To the teacher?

3. Name a specific subject area. Now list the ways in which you could apply Programmed Instruction.

PROJECT

Definition and Description

The *Dictionary of Education* describes the project method as "a teaching in which students individually or in groups accept an assignment to gather and integrate data relative to some problem and are then free to fulfill the requirements independently of the teacher, who furnishes help only when necessary." The Project approach may be referred to as self-directed study.

This method requires teaching by units rather than by pages. The decision as to the nature of the project can be assigned by the teacher, or it can evolve from class discussions.

Advantages or Special Purposes

1. The Project approach covers all levels of the cognitive and affective domains.

2. Pupils can be involved in planning the Project, thus increasing interest and motivation.

3. Emphasis is placed upon *doing* by the student.

4. The Project method develops student responsibility and initiative.

5. The student develops greater understanding of *how* to learn.

6. This strategy permits a study of broader areas because of the individual efforts or desires of the class.

Disadvantages or Limitations

1. Projects are very time consuming.

2. Projects are often little more than busy work and, therefore, students may seem to be learning much more than is the case.

3. Students, due to academic immaturity, often make many errors.

4. Often the materials and resources needed to do an effective Project are limited.

5. Students often get sidetracked or go off on a tangent.

6. Helpful teacher feedback usually is not possible until it is too late, i.e., at grade time.

Guidelines for Maximum Utilization

1. Be certain that sufficient resources and/or materials are available before undertaking Projects.

2. Great care must be taken in the selection of the Project. Students should be helped in finding Projects which have meaning for them but which are also meaningful in terms of the goals of the subject.

3. Be sure the Project is specifically defined and understood by the students involved. Establish objectives for each Project at the outset.

4. Provide enough supervision to ensure maximum progress, but not so much as to rob students of meaningful learning experiences.

5. Let the students evaluate their Project prior to any teacher evaluation.

6. Provide an opportunity to utilize *community resources*.

7. Evaluate according to agreed upon objectives.

Summary

Projects are usually done by individuals and frequently take the form of a model or presentation as the final product. If a Project involves in-depth work, it becomes research (see *student research*). Well known examples of Projects are seen at science fairs. In geography, students may make globes, or papier-maché relief maps. In mathematics, puzzles, models, or games may be created. Sometimes projects are creative but often they are duplicative of something already done.

Projects give students the opportunity to work independently and to gain in-depth knowledge of a specific area.

Group Projects sometimes take the form of a large-scale city map, play production, jury trial, large model construction, model grocery store, etc. The advantages of group Projects are that students must agree on division of labor, learn to lead or follow, and give and take criticism among themselves, as well as learn together about specific subject matter.

Questions to Promote Discussion

1. As a student, what are/were your personal reactions to "doing a Project"? Explain.

2. What do you consider to be the major advantage of the Project method? Why?

3. What do you consider to be the chief problem associated with the Project method? Why?

4. What steps could you take to overcome or minimize the chief problem of the Project method?

QUESTIONING

Definition and Description

Questioning, sometimes referred to as the question-and-answer method, is defined as "a method both of instruction and of oral testing based on teacher-formulated questions to be answered by the students."

Advantages or Special Purposes

1. In using questions the teacher must first be aware of the purposes to which they may be correctly applied. Callahan lists the following classifications of the purposes of questions (Sterling G. Callahan, *Successful Teaching in Secondary Schools*, page 200):
   a. Stimulate analytical thought.
   b. Diagnose student difficulties.
   c. Determine progress toward specific goals.
   d. Motivate students.
   e. Clarify and expand concepts.
   f. Encourage new appreciations and attitudes.
   g. Give specific direction to thinking.
   h. Relate cause to effect.
   i. Encourage student self-evaluation.
   j. Encourage the application of concepts.

2. Aschner, in his book, *Strategies and Tactics in Secondary School Teaching: A Book of Readings*, believes that teachers use questions to stimulate four types of thinking activities. The types are: remembering, reasoning, evaluating or judging, and creative thinking.

3. In a similar manner, questions may be designed in terms of Bloom's *Taxonomy of Educational Objectives: Cognitive Domain*. Such questions may be organized to serve the purpose of measuring learning on the levels of information, comprehension, application, analysis, synthesis or evaluation.

4. In the instructional process, questions can serve as a means of feedback for the teacher. This feedback can be either in terms of the understanding of an individual student or the understanding of the total class.

5. Lastly, questions are sometimes used as a control device in the sense that when students know they may be called upon at any time, they are more apt to pay attention to what is going on in class.

Disadvantages or Limitations

1. Questioning is a slower process in dealing with information than the *lecture*.

2. It is difficult to design questions to measure certain types of learning. It is easier to design questions which measure factual learning than those which measure analysis, synthesis, and evaluation.

3. It is the ease of designing factual questions which leads teachers often to ignore planning questions in advance; thus most questions asked by teachers tend to be factual in nature. Students feel encouraged to memorize, neglecting higher learning levels.

4. Several incorrectly answered questions often prompt teachers to feel more time should be spent lecturing than questioning. This is partially caused by the threat to the teacher's ego. Who wants to feel he or she has not been successful in teaching?

5. Consistently answering questions incorrectly may lead to a lessened self-concept for the student.

Guidelines for Maximum Utilization

Whatever the purpose of the questions to be asked by the teacher, the responsibility of the teacher is first to plan properly and then to execute effectively. In planning, the teacher should:

1. Decide upon the purposes of the questions to be used.

2. Structure, in advance, the more difficult types of questions to be used. It is desirable to take the time to write out such questions on note cards or the margins of the text.

3. If questions are to be used for either review or preassessment purposes, be sure to sample class responses randomly.

4. Use "who," "what," "when," and "where" questions to check information possessed by students. For higher thought levels, use "why" and "how" questions.

5. Push students' responses to "why" and "how" questions to higher levels of thought by asking for more explanation.

6. When using questions with individuals, state the question, pause, then call on a student to answer. This leads all students to listen to the question. The pause provides time to think—respect that period of silence.

7. Summarize complicated or ambiguous answers to questions.

8. Do not embarrass a student by repeatedly asking questions the student is unable to answer.

9. Be reasonably lavish in the use of "good," or other words of praise to students who give correct answers. Avoid making any negative comments after an incorrect answer; this is the surest way to insure low response on future questioning.

10. Allow students the opportunity to formulate questions in response to answers from the teacher or other students.

11. Questions can be used in connection with games such as "Bees" or the class's own version of "Hollywood Squares."

Summary

An effective question-asker is as beautiful to watch (listen to) as a fencer. He/she knows when and what to ask. His/her questions demand thinking, not just factual recall. It takes a certain measure of ego-elimination on the part of the teacher to relinquish the desire to furnish all the answers and allow the students to use their own cognitive abilities.

Good Questioning techniques aid and stimulate the listener to reason, evaluate, and even create. Inspiration is given by the teacher for the student to move beyond memorizing thought functions to higher levels of thinking.

Very important, obviously, is positive reinforcement of answers symbolizing "good thinking" if one wishes it to continue.

Questions to Promote Discussion

1. Imagine a teacher instructing a class session using only Questions. What would be some outcomes of that session for the students? Explain.

2. What is the major difficulty teachers have in using Questions? Why?

3. How could you overcome the difficulty you mentioned in answer to Question #2?

ROLE-PLAYING

Definition and Description

The *Dictionary of Education* explains Role-playing as "an instructional technique involving a spontaneous portrayal (acting out) of a situation, condition, or circumstances by selected members of a learning group." The situation to which the person responds may be either structured or unstructured.

A mock job interview in which the student is aware of the questions ahead of time exemplifies a structured situation. Throwing unusual or surprise questions into the interview would be unstructured for the student and would require spontaneity.

Advantages or Special Purposes

1. In Role-playing the student expresses feeling and attitudes.

2. Role-playing encourages creativity.

3. This method provides the student with the opportunity to "feel" the situation rather than merely intellectualize about it.

4. The student is motivated.

5. Students are being prepared for actual situations to be faced.

6. How students fit into their roles gives an indication of their knowledge of the situation.

7. Role-playing can be used to develop social skills.

8. Affective learning can be taught and/or effectively evaluated.

9. A system of communication based on action rather than words is used.

10. Role-playing provides a chance to pretest ideas of significance for future reference.

11. One learns to organize thoughts and responses instantly while reacting to a situation or question.

12. Students learn to remain calm in the face of adversity or pressure.

Disadvantages or Limitations

1. Students sometimes emphasize performance over the intended lesson.

2. Role-playing is time consuming.

3. Some students are unable to identify with the characters or situation.

4. Those students with talent often monopolize the situation.

5. Students often get "carried away" in their roles, which can lead to disruption of the class or distortion of the learning.

6. "Hot topics" and controversial issues often get out of hand in Role-playing.

7. This method may be harmful to those students who lack the necessary skills (those who are shy, or those who have speech problems).

8. Role-playing sometimes turns out to be a "dud" if it fails to relate to the student or lesson intended.

9. Playing roles demands some imagination on the part of the individual students involved.

10. Role-playing may benefit only the actual participants unless the objectives for the class have been clearly specified.

Guidelines for Maximum Utilization

1. Design the situation being utilized in sufficient detail in advance of the class session.

2. Define the *roles* in terms of the situation, keeping in mind student characteristics. (Actually, doing both numbers 1 and 2 in written form will be worth the effort.)

3. The actors should be given a short time to get their thoughts together.

4. The class members who are to observe should take notes and be instructed in what to look for.

5. Upon completion of the activity, evaluation of the students' performance should take place.

6. Certain portions of the activity may be improved with re-enactment.

7. In a "hot" display in which emotions get out of hand, a simple reversal of roles can accomplish much.

8. An atmosphere of freedom and security must exist in the classroom.

9. Here are ideas that you may want to choose in using the Role-playing strategy. The creative teacher will also think of many others that meet the needs in a specific situation.

   Business
   1. A labor representative negotiates a sensitive issue with the plant manager.
   2. A businessman asks his boss for a raise.

Education
1. A teacher encounters an irate parent.
2. A hostile male student threatens a teacher.

Humanities
1. An atheist encounters an evangelist.
2. A contemporary poet argues poetic theory with a Victorian poet.

Science
1. A fundamentalist Christian encounters a biologist who is teaching evolution.
2. An environmentalist debates an energy expert.

Social Service
1. Two children tell their eighty-year-old mother that she is being put in a home for the aged.
2. A white policeman harasses a black in a ghetto (good for role reversal).

Role-play situations especially for children:

1. The owner of a factory that is polluting the stream encounters a fisherman; a stockholder in the factory; the mayor of the town where the factory is located; and a fish.
2. A teacher meets with an overactive student who cannot sit still.
3. A man with two noisy dogs in his backyard meets with a neighbor who doesn't like the noise.
4. George Washington meets with a soldier who wants to go home from the camp at Valley Forge.

To involve the entire class when a Role-play strategy is used, the following questions are suggested as a means of providing a class evaluation of the situation.

1. How realistic was the performance of each character?
2. In what ways could the roles have been played differently?
3. How has the presentation changed your thinking about the characters portrayed?
4. What was the objective of the lesson portrayed?

Summary

Role-play has a unique value in that it is the only strategy that gets the student into another "identity," thus allowing him/her an opportunity to perceive how others might feel, think and act. This is especially useful in helping students understand the circumstances of different ethnic and cultural backgrounds.

Another valid use for Role-playing is in a problem-solving situation where different roles are placed in conflict with each other. This is utilized well in teacher education preparation classes where scenes such as problem child-parent-teacher, or principal-teacher-angry parent can be experienced.

It is highly recommended that the role-players thoroughly understand their roles, the limits of the roles and the situation of the scene prior to enactment. This eliminates straying or turning a learning situation into a comedy.

Questions to Promote Discussion

1. Role-playing is often viewed as "fun" by students. How can you ensure that the "fun" is a real learning experience?

2. What is the major difficulty in using Role-playing in the class? Why?

3. What could you do to overcome this difficulty?

4. What do you consider to be the major use of Role-playing in the classroom? Why?

SIMULATION GAMING

Definition and Description

Simulation is an elaborate type of role-playing, gaming, and socio-drama in which students simulate models of real-life situations. It invites participants to develop decision-making competencies while striving for established objectives, usually using competition between two teams or achieving a score which can be compared to an established norm score.

Simulation games are produced by commercial enterprises (e.g., Zuckerman, David W. and Horn, Robert E. *The Guide to Simulation Games for Education and Training.* Cambridge, Information Resources Inc., 1970), but can be designed by the classroom teacher. Generally, the teacher devises rules and objectives to the game and provides roles for various students.

Advantages or Special Purposes

1. Simulation is appealing, motivates intense effort, and increases learning.

2. Success or failure is rapidly and readily recognizable.

3. Vividness, meaning, and potential for greater retention are added.

4. Simulation has demonstrated its power to generate deep emotional involvement.

5. Learning to act by acting, learning to make decisions by making decisions, and learning to solve problems by solving problems are developed.

6. Simulation is particularly effective with under-motivated children.

7. Simulation allows for manipulation by simplifying the complexity of what the game represents, thus providing for control of extraneous factors that exist in the real situation.

8. Simulation can be used for the acquisition of information, improvement of new processes, and identification of alternatives in decision-making.

9. Games lengthen the attention span and develop persistent application to work.

10. Optional starting and stopping times are distinct advantages.

11. Pupils learn to cope with unpredictable circumstances.

12. Games illustrate vividly the relationship between decision-making and its consequences.

13. The need for constant communication between players teaches social integration/interaction.

14. Games are effective in teaching values and attitudes.

15. Simulation provides for critiques of solutions, successes, mistakes, and decisions made.

16. The cost and time necessary for involvement in the real world are reduced.

Disadvantages or Limitations

1. At best, simulation is very artificial and oversimplified.

2. Games place too much emphasis on competition.

3. Models are too rigid and narrow in their applicability.

4. Simulation takes too long to get to the heart of a lesson.

5. Teachers employing Simulation may be looked upon as allowing too much freedom and disorder.

6. Games cannot be readily adapted to the peculiar needs of an individual or a particular class.

7. Gaming and role-playing often become activities for activity's sake and fail to provide for transfer; Simulation cannot be a substitute for real, direct experience.

8. Students who have minor roles lose interest.

9. A complex model confuses; if it is simple, it bores.

10. The features represented and the outcomes to be achieved are predetermined by the designer, who builds in his/her own biases.

11. Time factors involved in Simulation Gaming do not always coincide with those time constraints under which the teacher functions.

Guidelines for Maximum Utilization

If a commercially made Simulation game is used then you need to be completely familiar with the game and prepare your class by: a) allowing sufficient time for the play; and b) carefully explaining the rules of the game. All Simulation games include directions for play, summarizing the activity, and relating it to "reality." These should be strictly adhered to.

If you desire to construct your own Simulation situation, the following suggestions from Von Haden and King should be considered.

1. In order to produce transferrable results, the model must possess fidelity in its representation of reality.

2. Purpose and major focus must be clearly understood.

3. Rules for Simulation games must be established.

4. The sophistication of the game usually increases its instructional potential.

5. Game designs must result from rigorous experimentation.

6. Simulation of all types should be evaluated in terms of the established objectives.

7. Learners in games must be free to carry out their own decisions, even when making mistakes, and the feedback of the consequences should be rapid and clear.

8. Opportunity and space must be provided for free, uninhibited movement and for flexibility of grouping.

9. An open climate should be maintained, free from leader domination.

10. The scope of the Simulation should be limited to selected critical aspects of actions or processes.

11. Creativity on the part of leaders and students is required.

12. Accurate information and facts are essential.

13. Reasonable assurance for intelligent use can be increased by setting significant goals and by previous testing.

14. Simulation should provide for teaching both the cognitive and the affective areas.

15. In the main, decisions must be sufficiently satisfying and rewarding to provide adequate motivation.

16. Provision must be made for developing generalizations and/or summarizations.

17. The situation should be repeatable in its original form so that followup can be provided.

Summary

The greatest thing going for the Simulation Gaming strategy is its intrinsic motivation. All kids love games, competition, and "winning." Whether you feel this aspect is the major emphasis of Simulation or not, the children do. Failure to capitalize on this enthusiastically will undermine all the preparation and time you invested to get across the "lesson."

The most frequent problem is getting started, and secondly, rule interpretation as the game progresses. The teacher is crucial to both of these. He/she must act as explainer of the game's objective and methods prior to play and as a referee during the game. A great deal of the success of the experience rests upon how well this is done.

To introduce you to Simulation Games, three examples are briefly described. The game with directions, necessary equipment and details may be purchased from the publishers listed.

THE ROAD GAME   5th grade and older
Thomas Linehan and Barbara Long   18 to 35 players
Herder and Herder   1½ to 2½ hours
New York, New York   10022

Imaginative, open-ended game devised by an art teacher and a psychologist. Teams attempt to build (paint) roads through their team's territories; team leaders, chosen by their groups, do the negotiating. In addition to esthetic questions, players must deal with conflict and cooperation, the purpose of rules, group decision-making and leadership.

HUMANUS   Junior High and older
Paul Twelker and Kent Layden   5 or more players
Limile II   1½ hours
La Jolla, California   92037

Survivors of a world catastrophe are at the mercy of a talking computer (audio tape). To survive, players must make fateful decisions. Strong emotional involvement is possible.

DEMOCRACY   Junior High and older
James S. Coleman   6 to 11 players
Western Publishing Company   1 to 4 hours
New York, New York   10022

Democracy was developed for junior and senior high school students, but is also used with college groups and adults. By acting in a quickly established structure of relationships, participants learn something about the complexities of decision-making in a democracy.

Questions to Promote Discussion

1. What is the major advantage or benefit to be found in Simulation Gaming? Why?

2. What is the chief limitation of this approach? Why?

3. Does the benefit listed in Question #1 outweigh the limitation named in Question #2? Why or why not?

4. Should Simulation Gaming be used more often in the classroom? Explain.

SOCRATIC

Definition and Description

The *Dictionary of Education* describes the Socratic method as "a process of discussion led by the teacher to induce the learner to question the validity of his reasoning or to reach a sound conclusion." The strategy derives its name from the approach used by Socrates as he assumed the role of intellectual midwife.

The Socratic approach was built upon the assumption that knowledge was within the student and proper questioning and commentary could cause this knowledge to surface. Socrates, as teacher, attempted to follow the student's argument wherever it led.

The key to the Socratic approach is that the teacher's comments and questions must enable the students to discover meaning for themselves.

In a typical classroom situation, the teacher would use the Socratic approach when the situation arose. It would be necessary for a student to make a statement, often of a value nature, which could be further pursued. The teacher would then enter into a dialogue with the student, following the argument until the student had thoroughly questioned the answer and gained some insight into the logic used or the attitudes and beliefs held.

An example seems almost imperative to further explain the Socratic strategy. The following dialogue finds Socrates awaiting his own trial for impiety. He is seeking knowledge concerning piety from Euthyphro, who is supposedly knowledgeable of such matters.

> *Socrates:* I know that, dear friend; and that is the reason why I desire to be your disciple. For I observe that no one, not even Meletus, appears to notice you; but his sharp eyes

have found me out at once, and he has indicted me for impiety. And, therefore, I adjure you to tell me the nature of piety and impiety, which you said that you knew so well, and of murder, and the rest of them. What are they? Is not piety in every action always the same? and impiety, again, is not that always the opposite of piety, and also the same with itself, having, as impiety, one notion which includes whatever is impious?

Euthyphro: To be sure, Socrates.

Socrates: And what is piety, and what is impiety?

Euthyphro: Piety is doing what I am doing; that is to say, prosecuting any one who is guilty of murder, sacrilege, or of any other similar crime—whether he be your father or mother, or some other person, that makes no difference—and not prosecuting them is impiety. And please to consider, Socrates, what a notable proof I will give you of the truth of what I am saying, which I have already given to others:—of the truth, I mean, of the principles that the impious, whoever he may be, ought not to go unpunished. For do not men regard Zeus as the best and most righteous of the gods?—even they admit, that he bound his father (Cronos) because he wickedly devoured his sons, and that he too had punished his own father (Uranus) for a similar reason, on a nameless manner. And yet when I proceed against my father, they are angry with me. This is their inconsistent way of talking when the gods are concerned, and when I am concerned.

Socrates: May not this be the reason, Euthyphro, why I am charged with impiety—that I cannot always [agree] with these stories about the gods? and therefore I supposed that people think me wrong. But as you who are well informed about them approve of them, I cannot do better than assent to your superior wisdom. For what else can I say, confession as I do, that I know nothing of them. I wish you would tell me whether you really believe that they are true?

Euthyphro: Yes, Socrates; and things more wonderful still, of which the world is in ignorance.

Socrates: And do you really believe that the gods fought with one another, and had dire quarrels, battles, and the like, as the poets say, and as you may see represented in the works of great artists? The temples are full of them; and notably the robe of Athene, which is carried up to the Acropolis at the great Panathenaea, is embroidered with them. Are all these tales of the gods true, Euthyphro?

Euthyphro: Yes, Socrates, and, as I was saying, I can tell you, if you would like to hear them, many other things about the gods which would quite amaze you.

Socrates: I dare say; and you shall tell me them at some other time when I have leisure. But just at present I would rather hear from you a more precise answer, which you have not as yet given, my friend, to the question, What is "piety?" In reply, you only say that piety is, doing as you do, charging your father with murder?

Euthyphro: And that is true, Socrates.

Socrates: I dare say, Euthyphro, but there are many other pious acts.

Euthyphro: There are.

Socrates: Remember that I did not ask you to give me two or three examples of piety, but to explain the general idea which makes all pious things to be pious. Do you not recollect that there was one idea which made the impious impious, and the pious pious?

Euthyphro: I remember.

Socrates: Tell me what this is, and then I shall have a standard to which I may look, and by which I may measure the nature of actions, whether yours or anyone's else, and say that this action is pious, and that impious?

Euthyphro: I will tell you, if you like.

Socrates: I should very much like that.

Euthyphro: Piety, then, is that which is dear to the gods and impiety is that which is not dear to them.

Socrates: Very good, Euthyphro; you have now given me just the sort of answer which I wanted. But whether it is true or not I cannot as yet tell, although I make no doubt that you will prove the truth of your words.

Euthyphro: Of course.

Socrates: Come, then, and let us examine what we are saying. That thing, or person which is dear to the gods is pious, and that thing or person which is hateful to the gods is impious. Was not that said?

Euthyphro: Yes, that was said.

Socrates: And that seems to have been very well said too?

Euthyphro: Yes, Socrates, I think that; it was certainly said.

Socrates: And further, Euthyphro, the gods were admitted to have enmities and hatreds and differences—that was also said?

Euthyphro: Yes, that was said.

Socrates: And what sort of difference creates enmity and anger? Suppose for example that you and I, my good friend, differ about a number; do differences of this sort make us enemies and set us at variance with one another? Do we not go at once to calculation, and end them by a sum?

Euthyphro: True.

Socrates: Or suppose that we differ about magnitudes, do we not quickly put an end to that difference by measuring?

Euthyphro: That is true.

Socrates: And we end a controversy about heavy and light by resorting to a weighing-machine?

Euthyphro: To be sure.

Socrates: But what differences are those which, because they cannot be thus decided, make us angry and set us at enmity with one another? I dare say the answer does not occur to you at the moment, and therefore I will suggest that this happens when the matters of difference are the just and unjust, good and evil, honorable and dishonorable. Are not these the points about which, when differing, we quarrel, when we do quarrel, as you and I and all men experience?

Euthyphro: Yes, Socrates, that is the nature of the differences about which we quarrel.

Socrates: And the quarrels of the gods, noble Euthyphro, when they occur, are of a like nature?

Euthyphro: They are.

Socrates: They have differences of opinion, as you say, about good and evil, just and unjust, honorable and dishonorable: there would have been no quarrels among them, if there had been no such differences—would there now?

Euthyphro: You are quite right.

Socrates: Does not every man love that which he deems noble and just and good, and hate the opposite of them?

Euthyphro: Very true.

Socrates: But then, as you say, people regard the same thing, some as just and others as unjust; and they dispute about this, and there arise wars and fightings among them.

Euthyphro: Yes, that is true.

Socrates: Then the same things, as appears, are hated by the gods and loved by the gods, and are both hateful and dear to them?

Euthyphro: True.

Socrates: Then upon this view the same things, Euthyphro, will be pious and also impious?

Euthyphro: That, I suppose, is true.

Socrates: Then, my friend, I remark with surprise that you have not answered what I asked. For I certainly did not ask what was that which is at once pious and impious; and that which is loved by the gods appears also to be hated by them. And therefore, Euthyphro, in thus chastising your father you may very likely be doing what is agreeable to Zeus but disagreeable to Cronos or Uranus, and what is acceptable to Hephaestus but unacceptable to Hera, and there may be other gods who have similar differences of opinion.

Advantages or Special Purposes

1. The Socratic approach can be used in dealing with higher level cognitive and affective learning.

2. The Socratic method gets the student to think about what is said so that he/she can really examine an issue in depth.

3. The degree of teacher involvement can motivate the student.

4. Students are challenged when this technique is used properly.

5. The strategy is transferable in that students can pursue this technique in discussions with other students.

Disadvantages or Limitations

1. It is extremely difficult to formulate the kind of questions used in the Socratic approach.

2. Due to the spontaneous nature of the Socratic approach, it is threatening to the traditional role.

3. This same spontaneity makes it difficult to be prepared.

4. Students often feel threatened when a teacher challenges their ideas.

5. While the teacher is in dialogue with one student, the other students in the class may lose interest.

6. It is difficult to evaluate a student's learning.

Guidelines for Maximum Utilization

1. Prepare for the utilization of the Socratic approach by reading the *Republic*, the *Meno*, or some other work showing the teaching style of Socrates.

2. Begin by using the Socratic approach on a limited basis, preferably on attitudinal statements of students.

3. Assure students that you are attempting only to get them to re-think their ideas and that you are not criticizing them.

4. Be ready to shift gears if the attempt to use the Socratic approach bogs down.

5. However, do continue to develop skill in using the approach; this can only be done by attempting to use it.

6. When evaluating learning, give students the opportunity to show the logic of their viewpoints, and give credit accordingly.

7. Start with simple logic and gradually build to the complex.

Summary

The Socratic strategy enables the teacher to aid the student in examining his/her own beliefs, values, attitudes and their logic or inconsistency. It is a difficult strategy to master and requires a friendly "let's-look-at-this" relationship. If this atmosphere is not present, the teacher's questioning will be viewed as picky and critical by the students, thus negating the purpose of the strategy.

Questions to Promote Discussion

1. What subject areas appear to you to be most compatible with the Socratic approach? Why?

2. Select a subject area *not* listed in answer to Question #1. How could the Socratic method be used with this subject?

3. What is the key guideline to the proper use of the Socratic approach? Why?

STUDENT RESEARCH

Definition and Description

The research approach to teaching is defined in the *Dictionary of Education* as "an instructional procedure, the desired outcomes of which are achieved by setting up situations in such a form that the student gathers and organizes information, draws his own conclusions on the basis of data, and compares his results with those obtained by other investigators."

The student may conduct this research in a laboratory situation or a non-laboratory situation or a combination of both. The non-laboratory research is usually some type of library research, as in the social studies, performing surveys, etc.

The classroom focus of Student Research can be either upon the knowledge gained, upon the research skills and processes involved, or both.

Advantages or Special Purposes

1. Research conducted by the student leads the student to learn how a discipline is organized.

2. Student Research lets the student understand how a researcher in a particular field works.

3. Research by students prepares them to direct their own learning in the future when faced with a new problem, e.g., developing an organizational structure for solution-seeking.

4. Research personalizes education in the sense that the student can research an area of interest or concern.

5. Research can provide motivation as the student actively seeks answers.

6. In using Research, students must make judgments, reach conclusions, and report the findings.

7. By conducting Research, the student not only learns content but also develops various research skills.

8. The student develops a sense of responsibility by conducting research.

Disadvantages or Limitations

1. Research can be very time consuming.

2. Research may require more materials and equipment than are available.

3. Students, although initially motivated, may lose interest if the Research leads up blind alleys (topic too difficult, boring, or too lengthy).

4. Due to immaturity or limited subject matter comprehension, students may often have difficulty judging the importance of data acquired through Research.

5. Students can easily become sidetracked or go off on a tangent in conducting Research.

6. Students seldom get to work with primary sources or do original Research, thus giving them a distorted picture of what "real" Research involves.

Guidelines for Maximum Utilization

1. Decide beforehand whether the purpose of the Research is the knowledge learned or the research process or both, and so inform the students.

2. Be sure the necessary materials, facilities and equipment for Research are available.

3. Base the type of Research upon the students' level of research sophistication.

4. Insist on students keeping extensive notes as the Research progresses.

5. Make certain the topics to be researched are well-defined and understood by the student.

6. Build in checks or student progress reports to ensure the direction of the Research.

7. Spend time helping students develop research skills before embarking upon a Research project.

8. Build in as many primary sources as possible. Such research methods as case studies or opinion sampling can help.

9. Provide students with opportunities to share their findings with peers.

10. Decide upon evaluation procedures in advance and inform students of the criteria by which their efforts will be measured.

Summary

Research is highly interesting to some students and a total bore for others. Certain students thrive on the independence, the logicality and definitiveness of this type of individual study (in other words, Research is not for everyone). A teacher must spend adequate preparatory time with the student in the foundations of Research: (1) defining the "problem"; (2) gathering and compiling data; (3) posing tentative solutions; and (4) developing note-taking and recording skills, etc.

A student doing Research needs input and the flexibility to make contacts necessary for such input. This might be library time or first-hand gathering of information from local and state agencies.

The rewards of properly supervised and earnest carrying out of Student Research can be great: thought organization, involvement, increased motivation, activism, in-depth knowledge of a specific area, and feeling of accomplishment.

Questions to Promote Discussion

1. What do you consider the major benefit of the Student Research approach? Why?

2. Given this benefit, why isn't Student Research more widely used?

3. What subject areas do you feel most lend themselves to the utilization of Student Research? Why?

4. Select a subject area *not* named in response to Question #3 and tell how you could apply the Student Research approach.

STUDENT TUTORIAL

Definition and Description

Known also as the Lancastrian system, youth-tutoring-youth or monitorial instruction, the Student Tutorial approach utilizes pupils as monitors (tutors) who first learn the lesson from a teacher and then teach small groups or individual students (tutees).

Traditionally the approach has been concerned only with the learning of the tutees. However, the approach also offers a unique learning experience for the student tutors and this should be considered as a vital portion of the approach.

Advantages or Special Purposes

1. The tutor learns more since teaching is an excellent learning situation.

2. Since the tutor is nearer the age, skill and achievement levels of the tutee than is the teacher, the tutor can better understand the tutee's problems.

3. The Student Tutorial system spreads the talents and knowledge of the teacher.

4. The use of tutors assures all students of individual attention.

5. The Student Tutorial approach provides an economic use of time (in reaching all students).

6. The tutor can develop responsible behavior as well as gain leadership experience.

7. The Student Tutorial system provides a challenging learning experience for the faster students in class.

8. Advanced students can often be paired up with remedial students and aid in eliminating troublesome "learning gaps."

9. This is an excellent method to extend the *drill* strategy.

Disadvantages or Limitations

1. Since the tutor and tutees are classmates, tutees often resent being taught by their peers.

2. The tutor is not a teacher and is very limited in instructional skills.

3. Since the tutor usually lacks the teacher's depth of knowledge, the use of tutors may lead to "memorization" transmission only.

4. The use of student tutors removes the teacher from the actual instruction of most of the students.

5. The only feedback the teacher receives is through the tutor and may be distorted.

6. Since the teacher is not present in all of the tutorial sessions, behavior problems are apt to arise.

7. The absence of the teacher from the instructional situation may be a problem of legal liability.

Guidelines for Maximum Utilization

1. All students should be given the opportunity to function as tutors. Remember, all students can learn more by teaching.

2. Use a variety of techniques when instructing the tutors.

3. Aim at the higher cognitive levels in teaching the tutors. It is essential that the tutors have both breadth and depth in the subject.

4. Prepare both the tutors and the tutees as to the role each will play in the tutorial situation.

5. The Student Tutorial approach is excellent to use whenever a large number of students have been absent from the class (e.g., flu epidemic). This is usually a dead time, but you can teach those present and use them as tutors when the absent students return to class.

6. In using the tutorial approach, all students should clearly understand the objectives of the lesson. The tutees can tell whether or not they are achieving the objectives, and are thus able to keep you informed.

7. Quick measures of tutee achievement should be periodically used to provide feedback which will indicate the degree of success of the approach.

8. Unobtrusively observe each of the tutorial situations.

9. Careful pairing of tutor and tutee is necessary to avoid potential personality or discipline problems.

Example

To free the teacher and/or provide a different instructional angle, a good student teaching another student has proved quite successful. This involves the teacher, aide, volunteer parent or student teacher developing lesson plans especially for the pupil needing individual attention. Usually this method is utilized for only short periods of time and on the lower end of the taxonomic scale such as drill (memorization) in multiplication tables, spelling, memorizing poetry or play lines. The adult teacher maintains checks over progress or problems, and, of course, is responsible for evaluation.

An interesting approach which has as much, if not more, benefit for the tutor as it does for the tutee is exemplified by a program instituted at Walter T. Moore Experimental School in Tallahassee, Florida, back in 1970. A group of sixth grade students (whom we might describe as "undermotivated" readers) were paired with second graders who were in need of personalized reading instruction—mostly being read to, and being able to read for someone. The sixth graders, who had lost interest in reading, had not lost their need for status, and became very involved with the little kids and liked the admiration they received as the "big teacher." As a consequence, both groups of students showed almost instant marked improvement which continued throughout the rest of the school year.

Student Tutorial does not give the teacher "more time." No strategy does. A teacher has 60 seconds in every minute just like everyone else. Student Tutorial does, however, allow for a more effective allocation of time. While the teacher must still plan lessons with the tutor (if not for the tutor) he/she does not have to carry them out. This leaves the teacher free to work with small groups or the rest of the class as a whole. "Unplugging" the underachiever from the rest of the class periodically not only gives him/her the chance to receive an academic boost, but also eliminates the potential discipline problems associated with the student who cannot gain attention through class success.

Summary

The use of students tutoring other students has proven to be a valuable tool for teachers in countless situations. It enables the teacher to provide additional instruction to those pupils having difficulty while continuing to maintain an on-going program with other students in the classroom.

It may be considered a form of *behavior modification* due to the selection process used to designate tutors and tutees. The good student is rewarded by being assigned or appointed as a tutor. The tutee is rewarded by being selected for additional assistance on the basis of need, acceptable behavior, and a proven desire to want additional help.

Other sub-strategies can play an important part in the Student Tutorial program. They may have only a minor role when used by the tutors but nevertheless are valid points to consider. *Discussion, demonstration, drill, questioning* and *problem solving* are a few of the strategies that enter into the Student Tutorial method.

The mere fact that a peer is aiding the slow student may make the difference between the tutee's success or failure in gaining knowledge and assurance that he/she can do acceptable school work which will enable him/her to be a part of the total classroom learning activities.

Questions to Promote Discussion

1. What do you consider to be the major advantage of the Student Tutorial approach? Why?

2. What do you consider to be the major disadvantage of the Student Tutorial approach? Why?

3. When you weigh the major advantage against the major disadvantage, is the Student Tutorial approach worth using? Why or why not?

4. What could you do to minimize the effects of the major disadvantage of the Student Tutorial approach you listed?

TEAM TEACHING

Definition and Description

Team Teaching is an arrangement in which two or more teachers cooperatively plan, teach, and evaluate a group of students. Teaching teams may also include student teachers and/or paraprofessional personnel.

Teams may be organized on a departmental basis, an interdepartmental or interdisciplinary pattern, or on a grade-level basis. Most team teaching arrangements include instruction in large groups, small groups and individual study.

As such, the various strategies throughout this book are applicable to the Team Teaching arrangement. However, the peculiarities of the arrangement itself require that certain dimensions or parameters be considered.

Advantages or Special Purposes

1. Team Teaching capitalizes upon the special competencies, talents, and interests of each teacher.

2. Joint planning, teaching and evaluation by the team members stimulates the professional growth of the teachers involved.

3. Students may be grouped on an educational basis rather than an administrative basis.

4. Students will be exposed to several teachers with different backgrounds and approaches, thus providing an enriching experience.

5. The use of small groups and individualized study provides for individual student needs.

6. Large group presentations make possible more efficient use of time and resources (such as visiting speakers).

7. Teaching teams benefit the team members in that beginning teachers are helped by experienced teachers. Also, the more experienced gather up-to-date ideas from the enthusiastic newcomers.

8. The use of large groups, small groups, and individual study conducted by various team members provides more interesting and less monotonous routines in the area of traditional strategies.

9. Teachers get more help from the non-instructional personnel of the school such as the counselor, librarian, or media specialist.

10. Teachers have more time for planning, preparation and follow-up.

11. Team Teaching may be used for all or a part of the students' day.

12. It also adds flexibility to the school curriculum and daily schedule.

Disadvantages or Limitations

1. Team Teaching calls for special physical facilities to provide for large group-small group arrangements which many buildings do not have.

2. The cost per student of effective Team Teaching is often higher than for more traditional approaches.

3. Team Teaching is attractive and seems simple, but its actual application is more complex for administrators as well as teachers.

4. Teaching efficiency is often reduced by personality and professional conflicts among the team members.

5. Specialization on the part of the teachers may be carried to the point that the student loses sight of the whole subject or teaching/learning goals.

6. Large groups and a myriad of teachers may only confuse and alienate the student.

7. Team Teaching may in actuality be meeting the needs of teachers rather than those of the students.

8. The scheduling of large groups, small groups, and individual study is often extremely complicated and difficult to communicate without misunderstanding.

Guidelines for Maximum Utilization

1. Team Teaching requires understanding and acceptance by the administration and parents as well as the teachers involved.

2. Team members selected should be those who possess the needed personal qualities for cooperation as well as instructional competence.

3. Adopt Team Teaching on an experimental or trial basis at first.

4. State the objectives of the experiment and design the evaluation procedure in advance of its use.

5. In the planning sessions define the roles to be played by each team member. If a team leader is to be named, determine selection processes and job responsibilities prior to utilizing this strategy.

6. Provide time and resources for the team members to prepare thoroughly.

7. Large group activity is most appropriate to introduce a new topic or unit, to summarize or conclude a unit, and to provide information beneficial for the entire class.

8. Small groups may be best used to discuss large group presentations and topics of student interest.

9. Individual study may help students pursue areas of individual need and interest and develop the skills associated with individual inquiry.

10. Further utilization of Team Teaching should be undertaken only if the experimental attempt proves extremely satisfactory to all parties concerned (students, teachers, parents, administrators, board of education, etc.).

Summary

Besides scheduling and material arrangement the most important facet of Team Teaching is the personalities of the teachers involved. It is paramount to the success of this strategy that the teachers involved like each other, cooperate, and communicate openly and honestly. All the finest materials, plans and facilities will not make Team Teaching work if the teachers cannot work together.

In the area of communication, it is vitally important to student progress for teachers to confer daily on learner problems and achievements (based on the old premise that "two heads are better than one") and to plan assistance for or promotion of those areas.

Questions to Promote Discussion

1. What do you consider to be the major strength of Team Teaching? Why?

2. In the 1960s Team Teaching was the "in" thing. However, its alleged potential was never realized. What factors do you feel retarded this development? Why?

3. What is the most significant factor in the proper use of Team Teaching? Why?

VALUE CLARIFICATION

Definition and Description

Value Clarification is a process-oriented instructional method which has one or more of the following purposes:

a) To teach students that a particular value object should have a predetermined rating;
b) To assist students in making the most rationally defensible value judgment they can make about a value object in question;
c) To instill in students the ability and inclination to make rationally defensible value judgments; and/or
d) To teach students how to function as group members who are attempting to come to a common value judgment about a particular value object.[1]

Example

Purpose A—Teaching specific citizenship attributes as desirable; teaching that socialized medicine is detrimental; teaching that polygamy is evil; teaching that the United States is the best country.

Purposes B and C—Students are taught the following rational mental functions: 1) The purported facts supporting a value judgment must be true or well confirmed; 2) the facts must be genuinely relevant; 3) other things being equal, the greater the range of relevant facts included in making the judgment, the more adequate the judgment will be; and, 4) the value principle implied by the judgment must be agreeable to the person involved in making the judgment.[2] (Purpose B is concerned with these four processes in regard to a specific value object; Purpose C is concerned with establishing a general mind-set in the student with which to make future value judgments.)

Purpose D—Basically this purpose is centered around teaching students methods for resolving value conflicts. Six steps are involved: 1) Reducing differences in the interpretation of the value question; 2) reducing differences in the purported facts assembled; 3) reducing differences in the assessed truth of purported facts; 4) reducing differences in the relevance of facts; 5) reducing differences in the tentative value judgments; and, 6) reducing differences in testing the acceptability of value principles.[3]

As can be seen by the above descriptions, Value Clarification is a complex and multi-faceted instructional strategy. The most prevalent purpose is A, that of instilling a predetermined value judgment about a value object. It is also, interestingly enough, the most rejected purpose by most of today's authorities in values clarification. The major reasons for this rejection range from accusations of indoctrination to those of stunting rational thought processes in students. Any person going through graduate school is also familiar with the political necessity of sometimes espousing a particularly non-heartfelt set of values. The repugnance of such unenlightened teachings is the reason why Purpose A is ignored for the rest of this chapter.

Advantages or Special Purposes

1. A person who works to clarify values:
   a) establishes a more purposeful direction in his life, thereby increasing personal and professional productivity;
   b) has more consideration for fellow humans;
   c) is more reliable because he/she makes clear where he/she stands;
   d) gradually becomes more aware and discerning;
   e) learns to make honest and considered choices;
   f) is less affected by outside pressures and prejudices;
   g) makes more solid and defensible decisions; and,
   h) achieves more consistency between self-I-am and self-I-want-to-be.

2. A group that works to clarify values:
   a) illustrates to members that others have similar problems;

    b) gives individuals peer feedback and alternative problem solutions;

    c) establishes group solidarity and mutual trust; and,

    d) helps develop leadership potential in members.

3. The teacher gains valuable insight into the real needs and interests of students.

4. The teacher becomes more aware of the attitudes, values, beliefs, and motivating forces behind student thought and behavior.

5. Subject matter can be made more personally relevant when combined with Value Clarification exercises.

Disadvantages or Limitations

1. It takes most teachers a number of months to become adept at conducting successful Value Clarification sessions.

2. The temptation for the teacher to "moralize" (a definite No! No!) is almost overpowering.

3. Sessions, although potentially valuable, are time consuming.

4. An insensitive teacher could allow students to get emotionally "bruised" if conflicts that arise cannot be healthfully resolved.

5. Some students tend to dominate discussion, while others will take a "wallflower" role.

6. It is impractical (as well as undesirable) to evaluate in terms of establishing a letter or percentage grade for Value Clarification exercises.

Guidelines for Maximum Utilization

1. According to Simon and Clark, the Values Clarification process is basically as follows:

Choosing—
a. Lasting values must be freely chosen.
b. Values must be chosen from among alternatives.
c. There must be thoughtful consideration of the consequences of each alternative.

Prizing—
d. The value must be prized and cherished.
e. Development of a willingness to publicly proclaim the value chosen.

Acting—
f. The zenith of values clarification is acting on values.
g. True values will be acted upon repeatedly.[4]

These seven steps of the process should be kept in mind when reviewing the guidelines.

2. An atmosphere of trust is essential. Never use students' words against them or as a means of "rational embarrassment."

3. It is essential for the teacher to be a member of the group, rather than an aloof or authoritarian observer. Therefore, the instructor should make, "I feel . . . ", "I believe . . . " statements just as involved students are expected to do. Students will reveal to the teacher (and group) in direct proportion to the teacher's revelations.

4. The four steps[5] in the Values Clarification strategy include:

   a) *Build a climate of trust and comfort-caring.* This is a process of making everyone feel at home. Is everyone aware of where the restroom and water fountains are? Is everyone comfortable? Does everyone know what is going to happen and why? This helps establish the atmosphere of trust and concern for group members so necessary to productive sessions.

   b) *Begin with easy to answer, non-threatening activities.* This activity includes questions easily answered in public. This beginning procedure recognizes true values which must be

willingly displayed publicly. Some sample non-threatening
ice-breakers:

  i) How many feel that health food is better than
  supermarket offerings?
  ii) What's wrong with being "just a housewife"?
  iii) Should retirement be mandatory?
  iv) Should teenagers get an allowance? Etc.
  (Questions, of course, should be tailored to the social or age
  group involved.)

Attempts at clarification should be made even at this early
stage by asking such questions as:

  i) Does/should everyone feel this way?
  ii) What could be some possible results of this action?
  iii) Anyone have a different idea on this topic?
  iv) Could anyone defend the opposite point of view?

c) *Gradually probe deeper.* Before deeper questioning can take
   place, the leader and the group *must* feel at ease with each
   other. Likewise, the leader must feel at ease with the
   questions being utilized. Some examples:

  i) How do people act on what they value?
  ii) How should we treat people who act on values not
      generally accepted by society?
  iii) Do groups have group values? Some examples?
  iv) How do you feel about the way you act on your values?
  v) What values, if any, should be universally mandated?

d) *Issuing a challenge to action.* The most difficult part of the
   values clarification process is challenging to action. True, it is
   up to the student to choose when and how to act upon
   his/her values, but it is up to the group leader (teacher) to
   offer alternatives and challenge with questions *with gentle
   discretion.*

  i) So, you believe in respecting your elders—how are you
     going to act on this in the next week?

   ii) If you believe that health is important, what steps are you taking to preserve your own?

  iii) If you feel that education is so important, how do you plan to illustrate this in your own life?

  iv) If helping others is, as you say, one of the major human purposes, how do you plan to exhibit this in your life?

   v) If you believe lying is sometimes necessary, what kind of personal guidelines need establishing to determine when to lie and when it is inappropriate?

  vi) If you believe that charity is important, when are you going to help collect donations for your favorite charity?

A wrap-up to each values clarification session in terms of "What have we learned today"-type questions is helpful in solidifying personal revelations and decisions. It also provides a sense of real accomplishment which is good carry-over motivation for the next session.

Summary

Proponents of Values Clarification feel that it is a long overdue and vital part of education. They hope it will send forth a generation of truth-seekers who are strong in their honesty with themselves as well as with their peers. Some educators believe it is mere fad and doesn't "put-the-money-in-the-bank" as an educational and human investment compared to solid subject-matter teaching. Others, like the authors of this book, see a new potential in linking values clarification with subject matter to make a more personally relevant and meaningful curriculum than ever before possible. It appears to be the ideal approach to the "internalizing of subject-matter" problem we educators have been plagued with for centuries. We urge more investigatory projects in this area.

Questions to Promote Discussion

1. What do you consider to be the major benefit of the Values Clarification process in education? Why?

2. How could a teacher take precautions to prevent participants

from becoming "emotionally bruised" during the Values
Clarification process?

3. How would you defend the use of Values Clarification in your
classroom?

4. What are the advantages and disadvantages of instilling specific
values in students?

Notes

1. *Values Education.* Lawrence Metcalf, Editor. National Council
for the Social Studies, 1971, p. 4.
2. *Ibid.,* p. 18.
3. *Ibid.,* pp. 122–3.
4. Simon, S. and Clark J. *Beginning Values Clarification.* Pennant
Press, 1975, p. 35.
5. *Ibid.,* pp. 56–66.

PART TWO

TEACHING SUB-STRATEGIES

TEACHING TECHNIQUES WITH
AUDIO-VISUAL MEDIA

Have you ever noticed that the fancier restaurant meals have more garnishments, the expensive cars more options, and the elite apartments all those nice electrical extras? Many times its those "extras" that really *make* the meal, car, or apartment. Unsurprisingly, the same principle applies to a lesson being taught. While some teachers regard media as a superfluous frill, the expert teacher recognizes the tremendous enhancement of lesson impact afforded by proper use of sub-strategies. It can, and often does, make the difference between a lesson that flies and one that fails (or as a friend of mine says, "Will it 'fly' or will it 'flop'?").

There are some general principles to keep in mind that, if adhered to, improve sub-strategy selection and utilization processes.

1. No one medium is the best for all purposes.

2. Sub-strategy use should be consistent with teaching objectives.

3. Teachers must be familiar with media content—how they may be used most advantageously, the difficulty level in relationship to student competency, conditions of availability, and suitability to class size (large group, small group, individual study).

4. The sub-strategy must fit student capabilities and learning styles.

5. A sub-strategy should be selected objectively rather than on the basis of personal bias.

6. The physical environment significantly affects the results obtained with media.[1]

Procedures

The basic five-step utilization formula that has been used for decades is still a good one. It is the sub-strategy equivalent of strategy lesson-planning.

1. *Prepare Yourself*
   Prior to the lesson, listen to the record, preview the film, filmstrip, or picture set. Develop your "plan" with introductory comments, questions, evaluation items, etc.

2. *Prepare Environment*
   Arrange equipment and materials. Arrange chairs, desks, tables, lighting. Make sure ventilation and room temperature are comfortable.

3. *Prepare Class*
   Introduce the sub-strategy item, explain objectives, stress what is to be watched/listened for, and what learners will be expected to do with the information gained (discussion, test, enjoyment only).

4. *Presentation*
   Performance of sub-strategy should be done with proper equipment or material operation (focus film, adjust sound, etc.).

5. *Follow Up*
   Summarize, review, discuss, question, test or whatever plans were made to help "solidify" the experience.[2]

This five-step procedure is a fundamental one. It is not sacred, and the teacher should feel creatively free to experiment with variations. An example variation might be just showing a film without any guidelines or introduction, in order to get the students' uncolored impressions. A display of still photos on poverty can have a message with no introduction or follow-up. In other words, as is the case with most guidelines, they are meant to guide and suggest and not to provide restrictions.

Sub-Strategies Explained

Each sub-strategy is presented with a brief *description, advantages, disadvantages or limitations,* and general *application* statements. Again, these are general statements meant to familiarize and guide; and are not intended as iron-clad guidelines. Most teachers will be surprised to discover just how many sub-strategies are available for addition to their professional arsenal of teaching techniques.

Notes

1. Brown, J. W., Lewis R. B., Harcleroad, F. F. *AV Instruction— Technology, Media, and Methods.* McGraw-Hill, 1977, pp. 71–2.
2. *Ibid.* (pp. 67–8).

AUDIO RECORDINGS

Description

Audio Recordings include tapes (reel-to-reel, cassette, 8-track, and cards) and records (disc recordings). In the case of tapes, they can be teacher-recorded, student-recorded, or purchased pre-recorded from numerous companies. The fastest growing aspect of the educational media industry is that of pre-recorded cassettes, usually packaged with visuals and/or a programmed text. Equipment for playing audio recordings can be purchased at minimal cost and is operated easily by the youngest of students. Disc recordings and tapes are now found in most school and public libraries, although usually they may only be checked out by adults.

Advantages

1. Audio materials are the natural tools for teaching/improving listening skills.

2. Tape has high versatility and ease of operation for its relatively low cost.

3. Storage problems are minimal.

4. Material that is recorded can be absorbed faster than the printed word.

5. Recordings can be used by small groups, large groups, or individuals (and with earphones can be utilized by individuals in the midst of a group).

6. Foreign languages and speech skills are probably best taught by regular supplemental work with audio materials.

7. In elementary schools, individualized audio work not only helps tailor curriculum to specific student needs, but it also helps minimize distractions (children with headphones on are psychologically isolated as well as being on a short tether!).

8. Recordings are available in almost any subject area. A good source: National Center for Audio Tapes, 348 Stadium Building, Boulder, Colorado 80302 (send for catalog).

Disadvantages or Limitations

1. Teachers may have a tendency to overuse recordings and bore students.

2. Although costs are moderate, they may still be prohibitive for programs with small budgets.

3. Broken equipment usually seems to take forever to get repaired and returned.

4. Repair costs are becoming prohibitive.

5. Damaged disc recordings are irreparable.

6. Regular maintenance of machinery is time-consumingly necessary.

Application

1. Plan by establishing objectives *and then* acquiring the appropriate recordings.

2. Preview material and prepare an outline on the important points. Decide what you will do to introduce, discuss, and evaluate the recording(s).

3. Motivate students to listen by explaining objectives and evaluation criteria.

4. Start material only after making sure everyone is alert to purposes and is comfortable.

5. Follow-up the lesson with discussion, questions, and suggestions. Go over evaluation aspects again if students are to be tested at a later date (to insure maximum retention).

6. Some suggestions for different uses of audio media:

   a) Utilize pre-recorded and print materials in conjunction with *learning centers*.
   b) People involved in speech, drama, teaching, ministerial work, singing, politics, and radio-television broadcasting should be required periodically to furnish their instructor with tapes of their rehearsed speaking abilities.
   c) Allow individual students or small groups to make taped presentations on special projects.
   d) Have individual students who have special hobbies, areas of expertise, or unique experiences make an audio *learning packet* that can become a permanently available resource in the classroom.
   e) Have students make tapes of interviews (see *interview* strategy) of community persons, visiting celebrities, or local hobbyists.
   f) Record popular music from the radio and utilize in discussion of "what pop music is saying to us today."
   g) Have students tape their version of a radio show on a specific topic.

7. Keep equipment and disc recordings in good shape by regular maintenance. This problem can be reduced by training students to use the media properly in the first place.

8. Set up a code system for classifying and cataloging your recordings and set aside a permanent storage/display area for them.

BOOKS

Description

Textbooks and other books are often overlooked as media. However, they do communicate to the student and are subject to certain inherent qualities as are other sub-strategies.

Advantages

1. The information is permanent and usually well written.

2. Proper material is available for almost any reading level.

3. Books are reusable.

4. The learner controls the pace at which the material is received.

5. Books use color and appeal to the visual sense.

6. Books can be used to meet objectives of both cognitive and affective domains.

Disadvantages or Limitations

1. Books can be expensive to use.

2. Motion, if required, cannot be shown.

3. Some other instructional strategy must be used to make the information available to a group.

4. Many students do not know how to "use" a book to achieve maximum benefit.

5. The motivation to read is often lacking in students.

6. All of the information a teacher desires to portray through books is rarely located concisely in one book, but usually must be pieced together from several sources.

Application

1. Spend time occasionally to help students learn how to get the most out of a book.

2. Clarify the purpose, or purposes, to be served by reading a given book—or portions of the book.

3. Focus on problems which may require portions of several books to be read in order to solve the problem.

4. First, emphasize concepts in having students report on reading. Then have them present data or details which demonstrate the concepts.

5. Utilize teaching strategies which enable the learners to apply the information read in the book.

BULLETIN BOARDS

Description

Bulletin Boards are either stationary or portable (the latter being handy as room dividers). Most are faced with cork, facilitating the attachment of display items. They are often utilized for long-term (more than a few days) display of concepts being emphasized in class.

Advantages

1. Bulletin Boards can be used to stimulate student interest in specified topics of study.

2. Students can be motivated in an area of study by having them participate in constructing a bulletin board display.

3. As austere in decor as many classrooms are, bulletin boards provide an opportunity for increasing environmental attractiveness through colorful and eye-pleasing displays.

4. When only one copy of a map, newspaper clippings, or a chart is available, bulletin board placement allows a number of students to study it at the same time.

5. Group projects or reports can be displayed effectively.

6. Individual student interests, hobbies, photographs, etc. can be exhibited.

Disadvantages or Limitations

1. Bulletin Boards in public school are an excellent source of sharp objects for posterior impalement.

2. The constant need to do bulletin board face-lifting can be an unnecessary bit of busy work for teachers.

3. Good bulletin board preparation takes planning and time.

4. A poorly done bulletin board makes a room ugly.

5. If a board is used to display only excellent students' excellent work, it acts as a constant reminder to the less-able student of his/her shortcomings.

Application

1. Planning is essential for successful bulletin boards.
   a) Know what idea or concept you wish to impart.
   b) Plan the display by first making a sketch and list of materials needed.
   c) Involve students by assigning various responsibilities, including acquiring and shaping materials and actual construction of the display.
   d) Be creative in use of materials, colors and textures.

2. Make student involvement an enjoyable learning experience rather than an "assignment."

3. Take class time to discuss the finished product and its implications.

4. Change bulletin boards frequently, approximately every two weeks.

CHALKBOARD

Description

Historically, teachers could have any color of Chalkboard they wanted as long as it was black. Today the chalkboard comes in all colors, shapes, sizes and degrees of portability. Some have special surfaces that require a particular type of felt-tip pen rather than chalk. Most times, however, this medium includes: 1) a large writing area, 2) a writing substance (usually chalk), and 3) an eraser.

The Chalkboard is so common that not much attention is paid to maximizing the use of this fantastic sub-strategy, but by following the guidelines below, the potential of even the trusty old "blackboard" can be greatly increased.

Advantages

1. Availability. Most areas assigned for instruction are equipped with chalkboards. Also, if more board space is needed, portable boards of various types and styles are handy.

2. The chalkboard is inexpensive, especially when the usable life of the board is considered.

3. It is flexible in use in the sense that teachers may use it, students may use it and changes can be easily made through erasure.

4. Space. Lots of writing space is usually provided.

5. The chalkboard can be used to present more formally prepared lessons or for informal, spontaneous sessions.

6. Ideas can be dealt with at all levels from facts to concepts, from cognitive to affective learning.

7. Various colored chalk can be used to develop the topic, show parts or build associations.

8. A point-by-point outline of a presentation can be made on the spot with diagrams, charts, and other accentuations drawn at the appropriate moment.

9. The visual communication of the chalkboard directs attention of the class to the purposes of the lecture or discussion.

10. Ideas or topics suggested in discussion can be listed on the board, reorganized, deleted, added to, and put in final form.

11. Test or discussion questions can be put on the board and covered up before the class assembles, then revealed at the appropriate time. This can save on time and cost of duplication materials.

12. A number of students can do practice or drill work on the board at one time, allowing the instructor to give feedback immediately.

Disadvantages or Limitations

1. The chalkboard carries with it a "temporariness." Material put on the board cannot be saved or made permanent.

2. Chalkboards are often fixed in such a way that they are "too low for the teacher to use and too high for the kids to use"; i.e., they are not always at a comfortable height for all potential users.

3. Being fixed, chalkboards can put restrictions on the use of classroom space and classroom activities since students need to be placed where they can see the boards.

4. Problems can arise for students who have vision impairments.

5. With age, use of certain types of chalk, and/or improper cleaning practices, boards can become "cloudy" as they retain chalk dust.

6. Some teachers are psyched-out of using the board because they feel a lack of artistic ability.

7. Motion cannot be shown.

8. A teacher's handwriting or spelling deficiencies are most obvious when using the chalkboard.

9. Making use of the chalkboard necessitates turning one's back on the class, which can allow disruption (and it could be dangerous in some of today's high schools).

10. Chalkboard work can be messy.

11. Writing on the board can be "down time" and may break the class's train of thought and/or discussion.

Application

1. Be prepared. See that the chalkboard and erasers are properly cleaned and maintained. Insure that chalk is available in sufficient quantity; students get very tired of watching teachers search constantly during class for a piece of chalk (or eraser).

2. Plan what you are going to write on the board: a) keep writing to a minimum by using key words or conceptual diagrams; and b) develop topics by using the board from left to right and top to bottom.

3. Keep writing a) neat, b) large, heavy and high enough to be visible by all, c) brief, d) specific.

4. Practice writing and/or printing in a straight line.

5. Use yellow chalk on a green board, white on a black board, etc.

6. If your chalk squeaks, simply break the piece in half.

7. Learn to stand so as to not block the view of students as you use the board.

8. Avoid writing and "talking into" the board at the same time.

9. Put the chalk down when you are through writing. This reduces the chances for distraction, as you are not "tempted" to play with the chalk.

10. Use the eraser to remove errors or make changes. Using your hands only smears the chalk and may deposit oil on the board, which can serve as a dust collector.

11. In erasing the board, use an up-and-down erasing motion. Erasing the board with a side-to-side motion only enables the students to observe (from a most unflattering angle) the teacher doing something resembling the "twist."

12. When you are through with the material, erase it completely so that it will not serve as a distraction while the next topic is being considered.

13. Intersperse writing on the board with questions or verbal emphasis. Keep the class aware of what is being put on the board and why.

14. If important drawings or maps are needed on the board, a teacher is wise to save time by 1) doing them before class, and 2) copying a projection on the board (from a filmstrip, slide, or opaque projector) rather than "free-handing" it.

15. Chalkboard etiquette: if someone will be using the board after you, please don't leave it for him/her to erase. Another nice thing is to clean the eraser against the board too.

CHARTS

Description

Any pre-prepared graphic device or poster can be used as a chart. It can consist of drawings, graphs, words, pictures, cut-outs, etc.

Advantages

1. Charts are permanent and reusable.

2. They are portable.

3. Charts can be used for ideas ranging from the simple to the complex.

4. They can be used alone to deal with a single concept or as a part of a series of several charts in developing a theme.

5. They appeal to the visual sense of students.

6. Charts can utilize color to indicate steps or development.

7. Students can make charts to show their understanding of the subject.

Disadvantages or Limitations

1. Charts are often too complicated or too detailed to be useful.

2. Students with vision impairments may have difficulty seeing.

3. Motion cannot be shown.

4. Teachers feel they lack the artistic ability to prepare charts.

5. Charts that are big enough to be seen may be cumbersome to handle.

6. As information changes, charts become outdated.

7. Professionally-prepared charts can be costly.

Application

1. Plan well so that the chart fits the lesson.

2. Make sure the elements of the chart are large, neat, clear, and vivid enough to be seen.

3. Use a minimum of elements on the chart—avoid crowding.

4. Use color when it will help explain the material.

5. Avoid blocking the learner's view.

6. Use a pointer so that you will be showing the total chart when identifying only a portion of it.

7. Affix the chart to the wall, an easel, etc., so that you will not need to hold it. This will also ensure that the chart is steady for viewing.

CHART PAD

Description

The Chart Pad is a large tablet attached to an easel. It is written on with a felt-tipped marker, grease pencil, or crayon.

Advantages

1. Material written on a chart pad page can be retained for later review.

2. The Chart Pad can be prepared in advance.

3. Written material on the Chart Pad can be used by simply removing the page from the pad and attaching it around the room.

4. After a lesson, chart pad pages can be stored and used the next time the lesson is to be taught.

5. The Chart Pad and easel are light-weight and portable and can be used where board space is limited or unavailable.

6. Various colors can be used in developing the topic, which can be useful in showing steps, sequences, etc.

7. Students can use the Chart Pad.

8. It appeals to the visual sense of students.

Disadvantages or Limitations

1. A small writing space is available.

2. Chart Pads cannot be erased and "scribbling out" is a distraction.

3. Teachers often get "psyched out" because they believe they lack artistic ability.

4. Students with vision problems may not be able to see.

5. Motion cannot be shown.

6. The cost (over that of an already available chalkboard, for example) can be prohibitive for some tightly-budgeted systems.

Application

1. It is essential to plan in advance what you are going to write.

2. Write *only* key words or make conceptual diagrams.

3. Avoid writing and "talking into" the Chart Pad at the same time.

4. Be careful not to block the learners' view.

5. Use color when it will help explain the material.

6. Write legibly—large, neat and vivid.

7. Either turn over or remove the page when you are finished with it, so that it will not serve as a distraction.

CUTAWAYS

Description

A cutaway is designed to show the learner the "insides" of the object. The cutaway might simply be the real thing with part of the "skin" removed. Or, it might be on the order of a scaled-up or a scaled-down model, depending on what needs to be seen. Human anatomical models are examples of cutaways.

Advantages

Cutaways have all of the advantages of realia plus the following:

1. The student can observe the "insides" of the object, which are normally hidden from view.

2. The actual operational activities can be observed and analyzed.

3. Cutaways may be purchased commercially.

4. Cutaways may be home-made by the teacher and/or the students.

5. Cutaways may be reduced in size or enlarged in size for easier study.

6. Cutaways come in working and non-working styles.

Disadvantages or Limitations

The same disadvantages apply to the cutaway as to the use of realia, plus the following:

1. Cutaways can be costly when purchased.

2. Cutaways can be time consuming for the teacher and the learners when they are home-made.

3. Because cutaways are often larger or smaller than the real object, students may misinterpret the actual size.

Application

Cutaways are used in the same manner as realia, plus the following guidelines:

1. Be sure the cutaway emphasizes that which the learner should observe.

2. Use working cutaways when motion is essential.

3. Relate the cutaway to the true size of the real object.

4. Allow students to make cutaways when possible.

FILMSTRIPS

Description

Filmstrips are made up of a series of still pictures placed in sequential order on 35mm film. Each individual picture is called a "frame." Filmstrips are usually between twelve and fifty frames in length.

Advantages

1. A wide variety of commercially-produced filmstrips is available.

2. The generally high production quality of filmstrips provides visual stimulation and motivates the learner.

3. Filmstrips are easily stored. A "mountain of knowledge" can be stored in a small container.

4. Filmstrip projectors are generally available to the teacher and are easy to operate.

5. Students can use the filmstrip projector in making student presentations.

6. Pictures, diagrams, drawings, and charts can all be utilized on filmstrips.

Disadvantages or Limitations

1. Home-made filmstrips are hard to make; thus the teacher generally has to rely upon commercially-produced strips.

2. Commercially-produced filmstrips "structure" the lesson for the teacher.

3. Filmstrips are inflexible in making the presentation.

4. The "outdating" of a significant number of frames causes the entire filmstrip to become passé.

5. Commercially-produced filmstrips do not always turn out to be exactly as described in the brochures.

6. The room must be darkened, affecting both teacher control and meaningful student discussion.

7. In a darkened room, it is difficult for the teacher to read a script.

8. Students cannot take notes in the dark.

9. Filmstrips do not show motion.

Application

1. Preview the filmstrip to be sure it is in line with your objectives.

2. Rehearse the presentation to insure that you have enough time, you are thoroughly familiar with the material, the machine is working properly and all physical arrangements are acceptable.

3. Keep the room lights on and projector lights off during the introduction of the filmstrip. The same applies to the summary discussion after the viewing period.

4. Use only with concepts not requiring motion.

5. Any specifics which you expect students to retain should be reviewed.

FLANNEL BOARD-MAGNETIC BOARD

Description

Flannel Board, flannel graph, hook and eye board are all names given to a device in which certain fabric is stretched over a board or frame. Cut-outs, backed by a compatible material which causes the cut-outs to cling to the fabric, are placed on the board to develop the lesson.

Magnetic Boards are also used in the same manner as flannel boards. Cutouts with little magnets glued to their backs are used on a metallic surface.

Advantages

1. These boards are best used in lessons requiring a step-by-step presentation.

2. The cut-outs can be moved, rearranged or removed to show action or the results of action and changes in the relationship of the subject material.

3. Visualization capabilities enhance a verbal presentation.

4. Judicious use of color attracts the attention of the learner.

5. These aids can be light-weight and portable or they can be permanently fixed.

6. Cut-outs are relatively easy for the teacher to construct.

7. Students can make cut-outs and use the boards.

Disadvantages or Limitations

1. Small cut-outs cannot be readily seen.

2. Cut-outs can be easily lost.

3. The flannel board has for so long been used predominantly with younger children that it may seem "childish" to older learners.

4. Less spontaneity is afforded since the prepared cut-outs limit what is considered.

5. Space is usually limited.

Application

1. The lesson must be rehearsed in advance and all materials organized accordingly for use.

2. Be sure all materials are present at time of use.

3. Use color in a systematic way if it will help show the sequence of important data.

4. Do not block the view of the students.

5. Avoid "talking into" the board.

6. Involve students in making cut-outs.

7. Encourage students to show their understanding by having them use the board.

GRAPHS

Description

Graphs are holistic representations of numerical relationships. The three types commonly used are the line graph, bar graph, and pie graph.

a) *Line Graphs*—The line graph is the only one of the three types that represents two dimensions of measurement, one on the vertical axis and one on the horizontal. Each point on the graph represents a value in both dimensions.

b) *Bar Graph*—A bar graph can either compare the relative size of several items or the parts of a whole in relation to that whole.

c) *Pie Graph*—Pie graphs are reserved almost solely for showing the parts of a whole in relationship to each other. A common example is the "healthy diet concept," showing the percentage of dairy products, meat, vegetables, sea food, and fruit that should be consumed for best health.

Advantages

1. Mathematical or proportional relationships in sets of data can be quickly and accurately perceived by the viewer.

2. A graph can be constructed with very little effort and/or artistic talent.

3. Graphs can be done in different colors or shadings to include a third dimension or quality.

Disadvantages or Limitations

1. Care must be taken that pictorial representation doesn't oversimplify and, therefore, inaccurately depict complex data.

2. Planning and preparation take time and special materials such as graph paper, colored pens, straightedge, posterboard.

Application

1. Before preparing a graph, decide specifically what it is that is to be portrayed.

2. Keep graphs simple but accurate.

3. Utilize different colors and textures for more eye-catching representation.

4. Make the total chart *self*-explanatory. All information should be on the graph so that it can be understood without narration.

5. If symbols are used, make sure they are clearly defined.

HANDOUTS

Description

Materials to aid in communication—such as outlines, case studies, problems, data, and summaries—are given to each student, usually for personal retention.

Advantages

1. Each student has an easy-to-see, permanent copy of the material.

2. The material is given to the student in some organized manner.

3. Information presented in this manner can stimulate thought or provide the basis for students to review at their leisure.

4. Information contained in Handouts can readily serve as the basis for group discussion.

5. Having materials in the hands enhances visual sense appeal.

6. The learner with a visual impairment is less handicapped.

7. Handouts can be re-usable.

8. Can be used with any size group.

9. It is possible to design Handouts to require active learner participation.

Disadvantages or Limitations

1. It takes class time for students to read the material.

2. Confusion and disorder can occur while the Handouts are being distributed.

3. Students may be reading the Handouts when they should be doing something else.

4. If a Handout is to be used over a number of days, some students may forget or lose theirs.

5. Spelling errors, "typos," may not create a very positive student feeling toward the teacher's language arts abilities.

6. Competent typing skills and duplicating equipment may not be readily available to the teacher.

7. It is difficult to use color.

Application

1. Plan Handouts in advance so that they are properly tied-in with the subject.

2. Be sure your Handouts are neat and accurate.

3. Be certain you have enough copies, and a few extras for replacing "lost" copies.

4. Tell the students what use they are to make of the Handouts when they are received.

5. Pass out the printed material only when you are ready for the learners to begin reading immediately.

6. Avoid talking while distributing the Handouts (in a pre-determined, systematic fashion).

MOCK-UPS

Description

A mock-up is an unscaled replica designed to simplify and clarify the workings of the object. The mock-up, which may be larger or smaller than the real thing, is generally constructed to show the "essential" parts and their functional relationship. A popular mock-up is the large replica flower with detachable parts that is to be found in many classrooms.

Advantages

Mock-ups have all of the advantages of *realia* plus the following:

1. Mock-ups permit the observation of essential functions of the object.

2. Mock-ups can be made by the teacher and/or students, as well as purchased commercially.

3. By eliminating unnecessary details, the mock-up enables the learner to zero in on the material to be learned.

4. Mock-ups can be made larger or smaller than the real thing.

5. Mock-ups are generally working types which stress the actual operations involved in the functioning of the real object.

6. Having students build mock-ups enhances the learning sought.

Disadvantages or Limitations

In general, mock-ups have the same limitations as *realia* plus the following disadvantages:

1. Mock-ups can be costly when purchased.

2. Making mock-ups can be time consuming for the teacher or the class.

3. Because mock-ups are not to scale, and because the parts may be in a functional arrangement rather than actual order, students may not recognize the real object when faced with it.

4. Students need guidance in the construction of mock-ups.

Application

Using mock-ups includes all of the guidelines for the use of *models* plus the following:

1. Be sure the mock-up truly illustrates the functional factors of the real thing.

2. Have the students make mock-ups according to a planned sequence.

3. Be certain to give the students a picture of the scale and location of parts on the real thing.

4. Use mock-ups when it is essential for students to "see" how the real thing works.

MODELS OF REALIA

Description

Often the real thing cannot be used in the classroom. If this is due to size—either too large or too small an object—a scaled replica called a model can be used. Models are near-perfect replicas of the real thing. They are either reduced in scale or enlarged in scale. Examples of models are: train sets; model cars and planes; and doll houses and furniture.

Advantages

Models have all of the advantages of *realia* plus the following:

1. Models enable the teacher to use items even when the real item is impractical due to size.

2. Models can be purchased from commercial firms or they can be homemade by the teacher and/or the students.

3. Having students make models enhances learning as well as providing motivation.

4. When students make models, many subject areas are combined in an inter-disciplinary manner.

5. Models come in working or non-working modes.

Disadvantages or Limitations

Models have the same deficiencies as the use of *realia* plus the following:

1. Buying models, especially working models, can be costly.

2. Producing home-made models can be costly as well as very time consuming.

3. Since models are built to a scale, students may misinterpret the actual size of the object.

Application

Using models, follow the same guidelines as when using *realia*, plus the following:

1. Present the model in such a manner as to help the learner understand the size of the real object.

2. Be sure the model is in definite proportion to the real object, of the same color, etc.

3. Use working models when movement is essential to understanding the lesson.

MOTION PICTURES

Description

Motion Pictures come in the forms of film (8mm and 16mm), video tape, and 8mm loops and cartridges. They are rentable and, of course, easily purchased.

Advantages

1. Motion Pictures are inherently high in motivation.

2. Motion Pictures are useful in showing movement or relationships.

3. They are adaptable for individuals, small and large groups.

4. Insure a consistency in material presented.

5. Require very little reading skill to absorb the contained message.

6. Motion Pictures are available on almost any topic desired.

7. Student production of motion pictures, whether film or video tape, is an excellent project method.

Disadvantages or Limitations

1. Locating films with exact content desired can be a problem, and getting them on the date needed is usually about a 50-50 chance.

2. Purchasing cost of films is usually too high for small institutions. Rental fees can also be rather substantial.

3. Previewing films on a rental basis is nearly impossible (for free).

4. Projection equipment is expensive and so is its maintenance.

5. The industry is changing so rapidly that some video equipment could become obsolete quickly.

6. Mechanical and operational problems are not infrequent with projection equipment.

Application

1. In purchasing, renting or borrowing motion pictures, order far enough in advance to allow time for confirmation. This prevents being caught short on the day you plan to show them.

2. Become thoroughly acquainted with motion picture content. Make notes of important terms, concepts and facts, plus discussion and evaluation questions.

3. Set up film or video tape *prior* to class.

4. Before showing, discuss with the class the objectives of the film or tape, important terms, and questions to be answered by the use of this sub-strategy.

5. Show the motion picture with proper attention to viewer comfort: seating, temperature, ventilation, and lighting.

6. After the showing, lead discussion on previously established terms, concepts, facts, and questions.

7. Tie the film or tape in with content currently being studied.

OPAQUE PROJECTOR

Description

The opaque projector is used to project photographs, drawings, book pages and the like onto a screen for group viewing. It performs this function by lamp illumination of the material with the image being reflected by a mirror through a lens onto a screen.

Advantages

1. Materials such as pictures which lose much in reproduction processes can be viewed naturally.

2. Color can be projected.

3. Small objects are magnified so they can be viewed by a group.

4. "Valuable" prints, pictures, etc. can be viewed with minimum damage due to handling by people.

5. Tracings and enlargements of printed or pictured materials can be made by projecting on a blank sheet of paper.

Disadvantages or Limitations

1. Opaque projectors are relatively heavy and bulky.

2. The room usually needs to be very dark.

3. Heat can damage the materials used in the projector.

4. Opaque projectors are expensive.

Application

1. Since opaque projectors are usually scarce, be sure to reserve one for the day you plan to use it.

2. Besides scarcity, the opaque projector may be in need of repair; thus the teacher should always have a Plan B just in case.

3. Practice with the projector in advance of the lesson so that the machine is properly placed to ensure maximum viewing effectiveness.

4. Pictures must be flat or parts of the image will be out of focus.

5. As with all sub-strategies, the material must fit the presentation.

OVERHEAD TRANSPARENCIES

Description

The overhead projector, by means of light passsage through a transparency, enables the instructor to project pictures and drawings large enough for use with a group.

Advantages

1. The teacher can maintain eye contact while using the overhead.

2. Transparencies can be made professionally or by the teacher.

3. Color can be used.

4. Transparencies may be written on and then the writing can be removed afterwards.

5. Transparencies are easy to prepare.

6. Overlays can be used for sequenced presentations.

7. Transparencies are reusable.

8. They can be used with both large and small groups.

9. Transparencies can be used with normal room lighting.

10. Overhead projectors are simple to operate.

Disadvantages or Limitations

1. The overhead projector, while educationally a bargain, costs money, especially if each classroom is to have one.

2. As with any mechanical device, moving the projector around can result in damage.

3. Occasionally, transparencies become overheated, causing them to be damaged.

4. Professionally prepared transparencies cannot be easily modified as information changes.

5. The process of getting the projection image at a height where all can see often produces a "keystoning" effect.

Application

1. Make sure the overhead projector is available when you need it.

2. Have your transparencies prepared and organized in advance of their use.

3. Turn the projector off when changing transparencies so as to not distract the viewers.

4. Use a pencil or a small pointer to point out important information directly on the transparency.

5. Overall, a cellophane roll or blank sheets of acetate can be used in the same way as the chalkboard.

6. Students should be encouraged to learn to use the overhead in making student presentations.

PICTURES

Description

The term "pictures" refers to flat, opaque, still pictures which may be photographs or pictures from magazines, books, or newspapers.

Teachers often use pictures in one of two ways. One is to teach children to "read" pictures. The other is to transmit information through pictures. It is the contention of the authors that both the uses are always involved.

Advantages

1. Excellent pictures are available in limitless quantity and endless variety.

2. Pictures are very economical—often free.

3. Abstract ideas can be made real.

4. Pictures are effective in creating interest.

5. A tremendous amount of information can be contained in a well-chosen picture.

6. Pictures are more effective than oral or written statements alone.

7. Pictures can be used to trigger creative activities.

8. Pictures can be used as an evaluation technique.

9. Pictures can be used over and over again.

10. Still pictures can be used to reinforce previous impressions, to present new concepts or facts, or to form a basis from which to develop new meanings of abstractions.

11. Still pictures permit close-up detailed study at one's leisure.

Disadvantages or Limitations

1. Small pictures are difficult for a class to see.

2. Often pictures fail to present a scale of size or perspective. An 8″ × 10″ picture of an aircraft carrier gives no hint as to its size. A similar picture of a row boat could lead the learner to conclude that the row boat is larger.

3. Too many pictures used at one time distract and confuse the learner.

4. It is easy for the teacher to be attracted by a beautiful picture which teaches little about the subject.

5. Unless proper care is taken, pictures can get torn, mixed-up, or lost.

6. Too much handling of pictures causes damage.

7. An organized, usable filing system takes time to develop.

Application

1. Pictures should be selected only in terms of their contribution to achieving the objectives of instruction.

2. Pictures should be easily seen, accurate, attractive, well-produced, and contain the information being taught.

3. Carefully select the proper number of pictures to be studied.

4. Mount pictures on a hard paper and cover with plastic-sheet laminations or a plastic spray for protection.

5. Organize and file pictures according to a system which has meaning for you.

6. Get the pictures as close to the students as possible. Use an opaque projector if necessary for all to see.

REALIA

Description

Realia—real things—represent the actual conditions with which the learner will live. As such, Realia should be used whenever possible. Real things are available. The task is to locate them and put them to use in helping students learn. Examples of Realia are: insects; coins; rocks; plants; pets; and stamps.

Advantages

1. Experience with real things with which one will deal is the best learning situation possible.

2. Real objects are plentiful and available everywhere.

3. Real items can be observed and handled, providing concrete learning experiences for the student.

4. Dealing with Realia motivates the learner.

5. Realia can be used as part of the evaluation system.

6. Realia learning can be extended through the use of classroom or schoolwide displays.

Disadvantages or Limitations

1. Real things are not always readily available.

2. Realia are not always practical for use in the classroom:
   a. Size—a real object may be too large (a submarine) or too small (a single human cell) for classroom study.

b. Potential hazards—Realia such as live animals, certain electrical and mechanical equipment, etc., can represent potential hazards for the learner and the teacher.

c. Cost—real objects often are expensive.

d. Need to maintain original structure—while some Realia can be dismantled, many others cannot be; e.g., cutting open a person to see how the heart functions.

3. Affective learning is hard to facilitate through Realia.

4. If left sitting around the classroom, the Realia can be a distraction.

5. Storage and retrieval can be problems.

Application

1. Be certain the real object enhances your objectives.

2. Make whatever advanced arrangements are necessary for proper use of the Realia.

3. Costs can often be minimized by borrowing real items from members of the community.

4. Keep the Realia under wraps until you are ready to use them; after using, remove the potential distractor from sight.

5. Students should be encouraged to help in locating and acquiring Realia for classroom use.

6. Develop a system of storage and retrieval which will be functional.

SIMULATION DEVICES

Description

Simulation Devices are designed to give the student a set of experiences under near real-to-life conditions. Simulations, long used in military and business, are gaining more use in schools now. Some of the devices used include: driver trainers, telephone kits, and mannequins for artificial respiration and cardiopulmonary recuscitation (CPR).

Advantages

Simulation Devices have the same strengths as *realia* plus the following:

1. Learning experiences can be held in the classroom or simulator laboratory rather than away from the school.

2. Students can practice in complete safety to themselves, others and the equipment.

3. Feedback is presented to the teacher and learner through behavior-recording instruments.

4. Learning by doing is usually faster and provides better retention than "book-learning."

5. Simulation provides the opportunity to function under "normal" and "abnormal" conditions.

Disadvantages or Limitations

Simulation Devices share the same weaknesses as *realia* plus the following:

1. Simulation Devices are usually extremely expensive.

2. Since Simulation Devices often are electronic in nature, school systems may not be able to provide maintenance services locally.

3. Some Simulation Devices are rather sensitive and break down under student use or abuse.

4. Simulation may provide a sense of "false" security for the student since mistakes do not lead to the same type of consequences as in real life.

Application

Simulation Devices should be used in the same ways as *realia,* plus the following:

1. Be sure students realize the limitations of simulation in regard to real-life consequences.

2. Stress the use of feedback devices for students as a means to improve performance.

3. Encourage students to use and maintain the condition of these devices properly.

4. Become aware of normal maintenance practices and procedures and apply them as required.

5. Use Simulation Devices to *enhance* instruction and not as a means to do all of the instruction.

SLIDES

Description

Slides are individual pictures which are projected on a screen for a class to view. Slides can be used with or without sound. The use of slides with sound is covered in the *slide tape* sub-strategy.

Advantages

1. Slides add realism to class presentations.

2. Slides can be home-made to fit the teacher's needs or purchased from a commercial outfit.

3. Slides are small, thus storage is not a problem.

4. Slide projectors are usually available to teachers.

5. Slide projectors are portable and relatively inexpensive.

6. All kinds of pictures, drawings, charts and diagrams can be put on Slides.

7. Remote control of the slide projector is often available, permitting the teacher to move about the room.

8. Automatic focus is often available on slide projectors.

9. Slides are flexible in that various sequential arrangements can be made to fit the situation.

10. Slides can readily be updated by simple replacement.

Disadvantages or Limitations

1. Since Slides usually are not captioned, the teacher must help students understand the material being viewed.

2. Because they are small and separate, Slides can be easily lost or become disarranged.

3. A great deal of preparation and rehearsal time is required.

4. The room generally needs to be darkened, thus causing the teacher to lose eye contact.

5. Too many Slides or a too rapid succession of Slides can be distracting.

6. Focused discussion is often difficult in a darkened room.

7. Teachers may lack the skill or knowledge to make Slides.

8. Commercially produced Slides may not treat the subject matter in exactly the same manner as done by the teacher.

9. Students cannot take notes in a darkened room.

Application

1. Prepare by planning subject and organizing and numbering slides.

2. Rehearse your presentation to ensure the best utilization of time, understanding of the material, proper lighting, and functioning of the machine.

3. If you need to rely on notes in a darkened room, use a small flashlight, directed so as not to reflect in the students' eyes.

4. Speak about an image only while it is on the screen.

5. Use proper pacing of Slides, approximately 3–5 Slides per min.

6. Use a pointer to indicate details you want the viewers to observe more closely.

7. Since the slide projector can get hot, keep the projector off and the room lights on at the beginning while introducing the lesson and at the end while conducting the summary.

8. Any lists or other information which students should have noted should be reviewed or presented on a handout.

SLIDE-TAPES

Description

The Slide-tape sub-strategy involves the projection of individual pictures on a screen with an accompanying commentary via audio tape. Although disc records are sometimes used, audio tape cassettes predominate.

The characteristics of the slide sub-strategy and the audio-tape sub-strategy are combined in using Slide-tapes. Therefore, only the unique features of the Slide-tape combination will be considered.

Advantages

1. Voice and/or music can be used to enhance the visual presentation.

2. Slide-tapes can be either of the home-made variety or commercially produced.

3. Slides can be advanced by a "beep" or signal from the audio tape, or they can be advanced manually by the teacher.

4. Slides and audio cassettes require little storage space.

Disadvantages or Limitations

1. The learner's attention can quickly wander from a taped voice.

2. Slide-tapes are less flexible since it requires modification of both the slides and the tape to make changes in the presentation.

3. The more structured approach of the Slide-tape limits spontaneous discussion by class members.

4. Because two pieces of equipment are used, there is twice the likelihood of equipment malfunction.

5. Using a manual slide advance with tape requires the teacher to "know" the lesson or to follow a script—which is difficult in a darkened room.

6. Automatic triggering of slides by a signal from the audio tape sometimes malfunctions, causing visuals and sound to get "out of sync."

7. Students cannot take notes in a darkened room.

Application

1. Plan in advance and rehearse your presentation.

2. Use live, personal narration rather than audio-tape if at all possible.

3. Be sure *both* the visual and auditory images fit your objectives.

4. Provide for a meaningful introduction and for a discussion time at the end since use of Slide-tapes precludes spontaneous discussion during the presentation.

5. Any significant specific data which you expect students to retain should be either reviewed or presented on a handout.

PART THREE

TEACHER-MADE TESTS

TEACHER-MADE TESTS

Most textbooks dealing with testing stress the use of tests to measure instructional effectiveness. However, most teachers use tests to furnish a basis for assigning a grade. Rather than become embroiled in a philosophical discussion—since teachers would still use tests for assigning grades and test experts would still stress tests as a measure of instructional effectiveness—let us say that tests can be used for both purposes. Also, they can be misused for either purpose.

Whatever the case, the several types of testing avenues available to the classroom teacher have inherent qualities much like the instructional strategies in this book. Rather than get bogged down in heavy statistical treatment, our aim here is to help teachers better use the testing avenues available to them. This approach does not preclude the need for teachers to become aware of statistics as applied to testing. In fact, all teachers should have formal study in properly applying statistics to the classroom situation on a scale not limited only to testing. That, however, is beyond the scope of this part of the book. Our focus is upon usage of oral, performance and written means of classroom testing as designed by the teacher. Each of these means will be examined in terms of its (1) definition and description, (2) advantages or special purposes, (3) disadvantages or limitations, and (4) guidelines for maximum utilization.

Before proceeding directly to this examination, certain testing concepts must be considered. These concepts will be used as criteria by which the testing means will be compared.

The first concept is that of *validity*. In test jargon, validity is often said to be the degree to which a test measures what it purports to measure. For our use in examining testing approaches, we are interested in what types of behaviors the various approaches best measure. Validity is the most important of the concepts since we must be sure we are measuring what we think we are measuring.

Next comes *reliability*. Reliability deals with the consistency of results in measuring the same thing. One way of looking at reliability is to expect each of a group of students to get the same, or nearly the same, scores on a test-retest basis.

The third criterion we will deal with is *objectivity*. Objectivity really deals with the scoring of the test. If, in the scoring process, the scorer's subjective judgment does not enter in, the test is objective. In this case, the student would get the same score no matter who scored the test.

The fourth factor is *comprehensiveness*. Comprehensiveness refers to the degree of sampling of what has been taught. Obviously a teacher on a semester exam cannot test everything taught during the entire semester. However, a proportionate sampling of the major teachings can be made. The wider the range of subject matter tested and the truer the proportion tested, the more comprehensive the test is said to be.

The fifth area considered deals with *practical matters* involved in testing. These matters include (1) the time involved in constructing and scoring the tests, (2) the efficient use of class time for testing, and (3) the ease of constructing, administering, and scoring the test.

As the various testing approaches are examined, there will sometimes be a focus on test "type" and then on test "item" at other times. The reasons for this will be seen as each is examined.

COMPLETION

Definition and Description

Completion, or fill-in-the-blanks, items are those in which the student provides one or more missing words. This type of question calls for the students to recall the proper response.

Advantages or Special Purposes

1. Completion items are best used in cases where the student is expected to recall specific facts (names, dates, places, events, definitions, etc.).

2. Little opportunity for guessing is provided.

3. Completion items are relatively easy to construct.

4. This item is more comprehensive than the essay type in that it provides for greater sampling of learning in the same amount of time.

Disadvantages or Limitations

1. Overuse of the Completion test approach often creates an overemphasis on memorization on the part of the learner.

2. The higher level cognitive skills are not tested in this manner.

3. While less subjective than the essay item, the Completion item still lacks some objectivity. The teacher often will need to decide if the given answer is "close enough" or "means the same thing."

4. It is tempting for the teacher to copy statements directly from the textbook, thus creating poor items.

5. Teachers often use too many blanks, leaving a vague and ambiguous puzzle to be solved.

Guidelines for Maximum Utilization

1. Use only one blank in an item.

2. Write the item so specifically that there can be one and only one answer.

3. Place the blank at the end of the statement. If this is difficult, write the item in question form.

4. Paraphrase sentences taken from the textbook.

5. Make a model with the correct answers for use in scoring.

Questions to Promote Discussion

Below are questions which contain some errors. Using the above material, identify the errors and explain how the items should have been constructed. (Cite the specific statement in the text whenever possible.)

Completion Items (Not necessarily parts of the same test)

1. A. Lincoln was born in_____.
2. Paraphrase sentences taken from the_____.
3. _____the blanks at the end of the statement.
4. _____only one_____in_____ _____.

ESSAY

Definition and Description

In an Essay examination, the student writes a response to one or more questions requiring an answer of at least a sentence. Such responses range from a simple sentence for an elementary school student to one requiring several days for a graduate student.

Essay examinations can be used to measure either content (the answer) or process (how well written) or both. The important point is that teachers often have not decided or have not explained to the student what "counts." Thus the student is sure to ask immediately before answering the first question, "Does spelling count?"

Advantages or Special Purposes

1. Essay questions are best used for objectives dealing with the improvement of written skills, interpretation and use of data, creative expression, organization of ideas, developing a position, and thematic development.

2. Knowing that Essay items will be used usually motivates the student to study more thoroughly.

3. While the construction of good Essay questions is more difficult than is generally believed, they are easier to construct than most types of test items.

4. "Cheating" or copying another's work is virtually impossible with proper use of essay tests.

5. The opportunity for guessing is almost non-existent.

Disadvantages or Limitations

1. Essay *items* are the most subjective of all of the test items. Their lack of objectivity has been demonstrated in research time after time.

2. With such a lack of objectivity, the Essay item is low in reliability.

3. Comprehensiveness of the Essay item is poor since a relatively little amount of material can be covered in a given time.

4. Large amounts of time are needed to score Essay items.

5. Essay questions are inefficient in the use of class time since the physical act of writing is much slower than the answering of objective-type items.

6. Essay items are not easy to score. They require reading time, and students have a variety of ways of expressing themselves, which demands more time for interpretation.

Guidelines for Maximum Utilization

1. Use the Essay means of evaluation only for those objectives for which it is best suited.

2. Decide whether you are concerned about content or process, or both, and explain to students.

3. State the question as *specifically* as possible so that students will know what you want.

4. Minimize the weakness of subjectivity by:
   a. Developing a model-outline answer against which all student answers can be compared;
   b. Scale the number of points to be awarded for each portion of the model-outline answer;
   c. Score all papers anonymously; and,
   d. When several specific essay questions are used, score the

first question on each paper before going on to the next
question, and so on.

5. Explain the reason why each incorrect answer is not considered
   correct.

6. Review, in class, the model-outline answer for each item and
   how you scored the papers.

7. Beside each test item, list how many points each is worth, thus
   allowing students a basis for gauging the relative importance of
   each question.

Questions to Promote Discussion

Below are questions which contain some errors. Using the
above material, identify the errors and explain how the items should
have been constructed. (Cite the specific statement in the text
whenever possible.)

Essay Items (Not necessarily parts of a single test)

1. Discuss the Civil War.

2. List, in order, the first ten presidents of the U.S.

3. Compare and contrast Communism and Socialism in terms of:
   a. the control of industry.
   b. the ownership of property.
   c. efficiency of agricultural practices.

MATCHING

Definition and Description

The Matching item is a set of two lists in which each item in one list is related to an item in the other list. The instructions given explain the bases on which the various items are related. For ease of identification, one column (the left) is often called the "statement" and the other (the right) the "answer."

Advantages or Special Purposes

1. The Matching item is best used for those objectives which require the learner to associate related data.

2. Objectivity in scoring is present in this item.

3. This item is comprehensive in that large amounts of learning can be sampled in a short period of time.

4. Advantage #3 insures efficient use of class time.

5. Little time and effort is needed in scoring Matching items.

Disadvantages or Limitations

1. Often, a sufficient quantity of related data does not exist to consider using Matching items.

2. When an insufficient amount of related data exists teachers often manufacture items, thus creating poor questions.

3. Instructions regarding the basis of Matching are often difficult to write.

4. Directions for marking the correct answer are difficult to write.

Guidelines for Maximum Utilization

1. Use Matching items only where a sufficient number of related data exists.

2. Items should be homogeneous. This means that all "statements" and "answers" must be dealing with the same thing (people or places or dates, etc.).

3. Explain the basis for Matching.

4. Avoid giving grammatical clues.

5. Avoid perfect matching so that students do not get the last answer by the "process of elimination," i.e., have extra items in the answer column.

6. Keep the lists under a dozen "statements" and "answers."

7. Arrange the "answers" in some order, generally alphabetical, to aid in finding the correct response.

8. Present clear directions regarding the manner in which the student is to indicate his/her response.

Questions to Promote Discussion

Below are questions which contain some errors. Using the above material, identify the errors and explain how the items should have been constructed. (Cite the specific statement in the text whenever possible.)

Matching

Match the following:

(Statement)   (Answer)

   1. Discovered the Law of Gravity.   a. Mississippi

   2. First president of the U.S.   b. 1976

   3. Longest river in the U.S.   c. Newton

   4. Largest city in Illinois.   d. Harvard

   5. First college in the U.S.   e. Chicago

   6. Bicentennial.   f. Washington

MULTIPLE-CHOICE

Definition and Description

With the Multiple-Choice item, the learner selects from among two or more alternatives the one which correctly completes the statement or answers the question. The incomplete statement or question presented is called the stem.

This item type seems to be held in higher esteem by tests and measurements people than by classroom teachers. Technically, the Multiple-Choice item is a superior item. However, it must be recognized that the item has some weaknesses which bother classroom teachers.

Advantages or Special Purposes

1. The Multiple-Choice item can be used to measure a wide variety of objectives.

2. Scoring can be done on an objective basis.

3. Reliability is generally good.

4. These items permit a fairly wide sampling of learning in a short period of time; thus they are high in comprehensiveness and efficient use of class time.

5. Multiple-Choice items are easily and quickly scored.

Disadvantages or Limitations

1. Multiple-Choice items are the most difficult to construct.

2. In constructing these items, much time is required.

3. Because test "experts" extoll the virtues of Multiple-Choice items, teachers often "force" material or objectives which could be better measured other ways into the Multiple-Choice format.

4. Multiple-Choice items are not entirely free from "guessability."

Guidelines for Maximum Utilization

1. Use Multiple-Choice items to measure only those objectives for which they are compatible.

2. Use at least four alternatives for each statement or question.

3. Write in question form.

4. Insure that each alternative is plausible enough to be at least considered by the student.

5. Avoid grammatical "hints" in the stem as to the correct answer (singular-plural, etc.).

6. Avoid the use of the word "not" in the stem. If "not" must be used, underline the word so the student doesn't perceive it is a "trick" question.

7. Avoid any pattern of answer position. Some teachers tend to make the last alternative the correct one.

8. Make all alternatives of near-equal length.

9. If you use both "all of the above" and "none of the above" in the same item, do so in that order.

10. Avoid using either "all of the above" and "none of the above" *only* when it is the correct answer. Use it at times when it is not the correct answer.

Questions to Promote Discussion

Below are questions which contain some errors. Using the above material, identify the errors and explain how the items should have been constructed. (Cite the specific statement in the text whenever possible.)

Multiple-Choice (Not necessarily items of a single test)

1. How many states are there in the United States?
   a. 50
   b. 48

2. A unit of weight is an
   a. mile
   b. foot
   c. ounce
   d. minute

3. The primary colors are
   a. red
   b. yellow
   c. blue
   d. none of the above
   e. all of the above

ORAL TESTING

Definition and Description

Oral examinations in which a group of established experts attempt to assess the knowledge of an individual neophyte are commonplace in the graduate schools of American universities. Below that level, however, the use of oral examinations is usually limited to the teacher asking questions of individual students in the classroom setting.

Basically, an oral examination can be concerned with either content or process. By "content" is meant that the substance of the student's answer is of prime import rather than how well the answer was said. "Process," on the other hand, refers to the manner in which the student answered the question. The concern here is for the development of oral skills.

Advantages or Special Purposes

1. The oral approach can be used for those objectives which require the learner to explain, tell, name, etc.

2. This approach is the only one which can be used to assess the learner's development of oral skills.

3. Only an average amount of time is required to construct questions.

4. Some students are psyched out by written tests and perform with more validity on an oral examination.

Disadvantages or Limitations

1. The oral approach to testing lacks objectivity in scoring. This is why teams of judges are used in speech contests and debates. The subjectivity of the scorer enters into the scoring.

2. Since this means of testing lacks objectivity, it also lacks reliability.

3. Comprehensiveness is low since the teacher can ask only a limited number of questions in a given period of time, thus limiting the learning sampled.

4. Class time is not efficiently used since the other students are uninvolved while one student is participating.

5. Good questions are difficult to design. Too often teachers do this "off the top of their heads," the result being vague and unclear questions.

6. Students often give poor answers because they lack oral skills, not because they don't know the information.

7. Giving incorrect responses or not being able to respond in front of their peers often impairs students' belief in themselves.

8. Teachers often are unsure of whether they are measuring content or process, or both.

9. Scoring is difficult because not all students have to deal with the same questions.

Guidelines for Maximum Utilization

1. Use Oral Testing basically to measure the development of oral skills.

2. If you must use Oral Testing for other purposes, do so sparingly and follow the remaining guidelines.

3. Decide whether you are measuring content or process. If you are not specifically measuring oral skill development, focus on content only.

4. Write out your questions in advance, being sure they are clear and unambiguous. (Refer to the *questioning* strategy for help on this.)

5. Make sure the questions proportionately sample the content taught.

6. Ask the question, pause, then call on a student. This will encourage all students to think about the answer.

7. Avoid a pattern of calling on people, alphabetically, down the row, etc. A pattern known by the students means one only has to think when his/her turn comes.

8. Do not make judgments on only one or a few samplings. You may have asked a good student the only question he/she can't answer.

9. Realize that any feedback you have received is limited since all students do not answer all questions.

Questions to Promote Discussion

1. What is the major use which can be made of Oral Testing? Why?

2. What is the chief weakness of Oral Testing? Why?

3. What would you do to compensate for the weakness mentioned in response to Question #2? Why?

PERFORMANCE TESTING

Definition and Description

In Performance Testing, the student is required to perform some physical feat or demonstrate some skill which has been taught. Usually this type of testing is applied to psychomotor learning. Generally students are tested individually although it is possible to measure objectives aimed at team or group skill development.

Advantages or Special Purposes

1. Performance Testing is best used to measure learning objectives concerned with skill development.

2. Learning is directly measured by having students doing rather than writing or talking about doing.

3. As students realize their need to demonstrate what is to be learned, motivation to learn is often increased.

4. Models of performance to be reached often improve the learner's performance.

5. Knowing the performance standard to be reached lets the learner work individually with efficiency to reach the standard.

Disadvantages or Limitations

1. Performance Testing is subjective in scoring. (This is why competitive performances are often scored by several judges, with the high and low scores thrown out.)

2. Lacking objectivity, Performance Testings is thus low in reliability.

3. Performance Testing is low in comprehensiveness because students are generally measured one at a time, so that only a few skills can be measured.

4. It is often necessary to put in a great amount of time to set up a performance test, especially if an apparatus is used.

5. Scoring takes time, especially to translate the performance effectively into a set of meaningful symbols for the learner's benefit.

6. Class time is not efficiently used since the rest of the students are not meaningfully involved while the one student is performing.

7. Discipline problems often arise among those "sideline" students not involved in the performance evaluation being conducted.

Guidelines for Maximum Utilization

1. Use Performance Testing only for learning for which it is valid: skill learning.

2. Demonstrate (or have demonstrated) and explain the standards of acceptable performance.

3. Explain the scoring system to be used and how each factor involved in the performance will be scored.

4. Keep the scoring system as simple as possible and based solely upon observable criteria.

5. Increase the objectivity of the scoring process by training student "verifiers" as scorers.

6. At the time of testing, have all required apparatus pre-arranged and checked out for operability and safety.

7. Define clearly what meaningful activity those students not directly involved in testing should be doing.

8. After the performance, explain to the student the significant strengths and weaknesses of his/her performance.

Questions to Promote Discussion

1. What do you consider to be the best use of Performance Testing? Why?

2. What do you consider to be the major drawback to Performance Testing? Why?

3. What would you do to minimize the effects of the drawback you listed in response to Question #2? Why?

TRUE-FALSE

Definition and Description

Basically, the student is presented with a statement which he or she must decide is either true or false. Teachers use variations of the item in which students must provide the correct answer if the statement is false (true-false corrected).

Advantages or Special Purposes

1. True-False items are best used for those situations where the student is expected to identify the correct alternative from among two possibilities.

2. Scoring this item is highly objective.

3. A great amount of learning material can be sampled in a minimum amount of time, thus contributing to a high degree of comprehensiveness and efficient use of class time.

4. Items are relatively easy to construct, but not as easy as is often believed.

5. Not much time is required for scoring.

6. True-False tests can provide the teacher with a quick means to analyze the degree of general understanding a class has of a large block of material.

Disadvantages or Limitations

1. True-False items are susceptible to guessing. Students have a 50-50 chance of guessing correctly.

2. Because of this susceptibility to guessing, reliability is fairly low.

3. Students seem to be less motivated to study for this type of item, perhaps due to the "guessability" factor.

4. While True-False items are relatively easy to construct, they are often designed without the necessary planning, which results in poorly worded items.

Guidelines for Maximum Utilization

1. Use True-False items only for those situations where two alternatives exist.

2. Use statements that are completely true or completely false. No "trick" questions.

3. Use short, simple sentences.

4. Paraphrase rather than copying directly from textbooks.

5. Avoid arranging an answer pattern which makes it easier to score, but can also be detected by students.

6. Avoid the hints given by statements using "always," "never," etc.

7. Aim for approximately one-half true answers and one-half false answers for a test.

8. Use "true-false corrected" and other variations to minimize the effects of guessing.

9. If the statement is an opinion as part of the question, state who is being cited.

Questions to Promote Discussion

Below are questions which contain some errors. Using the above material, identify the errors and explain how the items should have been constructed. (Cite the specific statement in the text whenever possible.)

True-False (Not necessarily parts of a single test)

—————— 1. Never punt on third down in football.

RANKING OF INHERENT CHARACTERISTICS OF VARIOUS

Testing Means or Items ↓ Criteria	Oral	Performance	Essay
Validity	For objectives concerning oral skill development	For objectives requiring student to perform feats or demonstrate skills	For objectives requiring student to develop written skills, interpretation, use data, etc.
Reliability	Low	Low	Low
Objectivity	Low	Low	Low
Comprehensiveness	Low	Low	Low
Time Needed For: Construction / Scoring	Medium / Medium	Low / Low	Medium / Low
Efficient use of classtime	Low	Low	Low
Ease of: Construction / Scoring	Medium / Low	Medium / Low	Medium / Low

———— 2. The Big Ten is the toughest football conference.

———— 3. Davy Crockett, who died at the Alamo, was once
governor of Rhode Island.

———— 4. In true-false questions, use short, simple sentences.

TESTING MEANS OR ITEMS, ON A COMPARISON BASIS

Written			
Completion	True-False	Multiple Choice	Matching
For objectives requiring recall. Student is to name, to list, etc.	For objectives which require student to select from 2 alternatives	For wide range of objectives and various levels of thought	For objectives requiring student to match or associate related objects or ideas
Medium	Low	High	Medium
Medium	High	High	High
Medium	High	High	High
High / Medium	High / High	Low / High	Medium / High
Medium	High	High	High
High / Medium	High / High	Low / High	Low / High

SELECTED READINGS

Alcorn, Marvin D.; Kinder, James S.; and Schunert, James R. *Better Teaching in Secondary Schools*. Revised Edition. New York: Holt, Rinehart and Winston, Inc., 1964.

Biehler, Robert F. *Psychology Applied to Teaching*. Boston: Houghton Mifflin Co., 1974.

Block, J. H., ed. *Mastery Learning: Theory and Practice*. New York: Holt, Rinehart and Winston, 1973.

Bloom, B. *Human Characteristics and School Learning*. New York: McGraw-Hill, 1976.

Bloom, Benjamin. *Taxonomy of Educational Objectives: Cognitive Domain*. New York: Longmans, Green, 1956.

Blount, Nathan S. and Klausmeier, Herbert J. *Teaching in the Secondary School*. Third Edition. New York: Harper and Row, 1968.

Brown, James W.; Lewis, Richard B.; and Harcleroad, Fred F. *AV Instruction: Technology, Media and Methods*. New York: McGraw-Hill Book Company, 1977.

Callahan, Sterling G. *Successful Teaching in Secondary Schools*. Glenview, Ill: Scott, Foresman and Company, 1966.

Capp, Glenn R. and Thelma R. *Principles of Argumentation and Debate*. Englewood Cliffs, N.J.: Prentice-Hall, Inc., 1965.

Chapman, A. M. *The Games Children Play*. New York: G. P. Putnam's Sons, 1971.

Chester, Mark and Fox, Robert. *Role-Playing Methods in the Classroom*. Chicago: Science Research Association, Inc., 1966.

Clark, Leonard H., ed. *Strategies and Tactics in Secondary School Teaching*. New York: Macmillan, 1968.

Clark, Leonard H. and Starr, S. *Secondary School Teaching Methods*. New York: Macmillan Publishing Company, 1970.

Cooper, James M. et al. *Classroom Teaching Skills—A Handbook*. Lexington, Mass.: D. C. Heath and Company, 1977.

Cribb, J. R.; Platts, G. N.; and Miller, Lorrane. *Dynamics of Participative Groups*. St. Louis: John Swift, 1951.

Cruickshank, Donald R. "The Use of Simulation in Teacher Education: A Developing Phenomenon," *The Journal of Teacher Education*, XX, No. 1 (1969), 23–26.

Davis, Harold. *Organizing a Learning Center*. Cleveland: Educational Research Council of America, 1968.

Dictionary of Education, ed. by Carter Good for Phi Delta Kappa. New York: McGraw-Hill, 1973.

Esler, William. *Teaching Elementary Science*. Belmont, Cal.: Wadsworth Publishing Co., Inc., 1977.

Fisk, Lori and Lindgren, Henry C. *Learning Centers*. Glen Ridge, N.J.: Exceptional Press, 1974.

Gardner, William I. *Children with Learning and Behavior Problems: A Behavior Management Approach*. Boston: Allyn and Bacon, 1974.

Garten, Ted and Hudson, James. "A Strategy in the Use of Videotape to Evaluate Recognition of Component Teaching Skills," *Audio-Visual Instruction*, May 1974, 22–25.

Gearheart, B. R. *Learning Disabilities*. St. Louis, Mo.: The C. V. Mosby Company, 1973.

Glaser, Robert, ed. *Teaching Machines and Programmed Learning.*
Vol II. Washington, D.C.: National Education Association,
1965.

Gordon, Alice K. *Games for Growth: Educational Games in the
Classroom.* Chicago: Science Research Association, Inc., 1970.

Grambs, Jean D. and Iverson, William J. *Modern Methods in Secondary Education.* New York: Dryden Press, 1952.

Hack, Walter C., ed. *Educational Futurism 1985.* Berkeley, Cal.:
McCutchan Publishing Corporation, 1971.

Hammill, Donald D., and Bartel, Nettie R. *Teaching Children with
Learning and Behavior Problems.* Boston: Allyn and Bacon,
Inc., 1975.

Hexman, Marie. *Simulation Games for the Classroom.* Bloomington,
Ind.: Phi Delta Kappa Educational Foundation, 1975.

Hoffman, Randall W. and Plutchic, Robert. *Small-Group Discussion
in Orientation and Teaching.* New York: G. P. Putnam's Sons,
1959.

Hoover, Kenneth H. *Learning and Teaching in the Secondary
School.* Third Edition. Boston: Allyn and Bacon, 1972.

Hoover, Kenneth H. *The Professional Teacher's Handbook.* Boston:
Allyn and Bacon, Inc., 1972.

Howes, Virgil M. *Informal Teaching in the Open Classroom.* New
York: Macmillan Publishing Co., 1974.

Hunkins, Francis. *Questioning: Strategies and Techniques.* Boston:
Allyn and Bacon, Inc., 1972.

Interaction Associates. *Strategy Notebook.* San Francisco: Interaction Associates, 1972.

Kaltoounis, Theodore. "Teach with Questions," *Instructor*, 82: (May
1973), 43–45.

Kaplan, Abraham. *The Conduct of Inquiry.* Scranton, Pa.: Chandler
    Publishing Company, 1964.

Kim, Eugene C., and Kellough, Richard D. *A Resource Guide for
    Secondary School Teaching.* New York: Macmillan Publishing
    Company, Inc., 1974.

Kratwohl, David R.; Bloom, Benjamin S.; and Masia, Bertram B.
    *Taxonomy of Educational Objectives, The Classification of Edu-
    cational Goals, Handbook II: Affective Domain.* New York:
    McKay Publishing, 1964.

Livingstone, Samuel and Stoll, Clarice. *Simulation Games.* New
    York: Free Press, 1972.

Lueck, William R.; Campbell, Elwood G.; Eastman, Leo G.; Ed-
    wards, Charles W.; Thomas, Clayton F.; and Zeller, William D.
    Effective Secondary Education. Minneapolis: Burgess Publish-
    ing, 1966.

Lundsteen, Sara. "Questioning to Develop Creative Problem Solv-
    ing," *Elementary English,* 51: (May 1974), 645–650.

McCloskey, Mildred G. *Teaching Strategies and Classroom
    Realities.* Englewood Cliffs, N.J.: Prentice-Hall, Inc., 1971.

Metcalf, Lawrence, ed. *Values Education.* National Council for the
    Social Studies, 1971.

Mueller, Daniel J. "Mastery Learning: Partly Boon, Partly Boon-
    doggle," *Teacher's College Record,* 78: (Sept. 1976), 41–52.

Popham, James W. and Baker, Eva L. *Systematic Instruction.* En-
    glewood Cliffs: N.J.: Prentice-Hall, Inc., 1970.

Postman, Neil and Weingartner, Charles. *Teaching as a Subversive
    Activity.* New York: Delacorte Press, 1969.

Rapport, Virginia. *Learning Centers: Children on Their Own.*
    Washington, D.C.: The Association for Childhood Education In-
    ternational, 1970.

Sanders, Norris M. *Classroom Questions—What Kinds?* New York: Harper and Row, Publishers, 1966.

Schlegel, Richard. *Inquiry into Science, Its Domain and Limits.* New York: Doubleday, 1972.

Shaftel, Fannie R. "Role Playing: An Approach to Meaningful Social Learning," *Social Education,* XXXIV, No. 5 (1970), 556–559.

Silberman, Melvin L. et al. *The Psychology of Open Teaching and Learning.* Boston: Little Brown and Company, 1972.

Simon, S. and Clark J. *Beginning Values Clarification.* San Diego, Ca.: Pennant Press, 1975.

Skinner, B. F. "Teaching Machines," *Science,* Vol. 128 (October 24, 1958), 973.

Smith, J. K. and Katims, M. "Reading in the City: The Chicago Mastery Learning Reading Program," *Phi Delta Kappan,* November 1977, 199–202.

Smith, Lawrence and Riebock, James. "A Middle School Tries Contractual Reading," *Clearing House,* Vol. 45, (March 1971), 404–406.

Stolivious, Lawrence. "Teaching by Machine." Washington, D.C.: United States Government Printing Office, 1961.

Sund, Robert B. and Trowbridge, Leslie W. *Teaching Science by Inquiry in the Secondary Schools.* Columbus: Charles E. Merrill Publishing Company, 1973.

Suppes, Patrick. "Computer Based Instruction," *Education Digest,* (October 1967), 8.

Sylvester, Robert; Middendorf, Jack; and Meinke, Darrel. "Four Steps to a Learning Center," *The Instructor,* LXXVI, No. 10 (1967), 73–84.

Thomas, John I. *Learning Centers: Opening up the Classroom.* Boston: Holbrook Press, Inc., 1975.

Van Til, William. *Education: A Beginning*. Boston: Houghton Mifflin Company, 1974.

Von Haden, Herbert I., and King, Jean Marie. *Educational Innovator's Guide*. Worthington, Ohio: Charles A. Jones Publishing Company, 1974.

Von Haden, Herbert I., and King, Jean Marie. *Innovations in Education: Their Pro's and Con's*. Worthington, Ohio: Charles A. Jones Publishing Company, 1971.

Wilson, John A.; Robeck, M.; and Michael, W. B. *Psychological Foundations of Learning and Teaching*. New York: McGraw-Hill Book Company, 1974.

Wittich, W. A. and Schuller, C. F. *Instructional Technology, Its Nature and Use*. New York: Harper and Row, 1973.

Zuckerman, David S. and Horn, Robert E. *The Guide to Simulation Games for Education and Training*. Cambridge: Information Resources, Inc., 1970.